/2017

THE

art of stopping time

PEDRAM SHOJAI, OMD

RODALE.

RODALE
wellness

Live happy. Be healthy. Get inspired.

Sign up today to get exclusive access to our authors, exclusive bonuses, and the most authoritative, useful, and cutting-edge information on health, wellness, fitness, and living your life to the fullest.

Visit us online at RodaleWellness.com
Join us at RodaleWellness.com/Join

Rodale books may be purchased for business or promotional use or for special sales. For information, please e-mail: BookMarketing@Rodale.com.

Printed in the United States of America
Rodale Inc. makes every effort to use acid-free ∞, recycled paper ♲.

Book design by Yeon Kim

Library of Congress Cataloging-in-Publication Data is on file with the publisher.
ISBN 978–1–62336–909–5 hardcover

Distributed to the trade by Macmillan

2 4 6 8 10 9 7 5 3 1   hardcover

RODALE

Follow us @RodaleBooks on

We inspire health, healing, happiness, and love in the world.
Starting with you.

To my wonderful family—Elmira, Sol, and Sophia.
My greatest desire is to stop time and be with you.

CONTENTS

INTRODUCTION   xi

DAY 1: Assembling Your Life Garden   1
DAY 2: Time for Gratitude   3
DAY 3: Nature   5
DAY 4: E-Mail Time   7
DAY 5: When to Lie Low   9
DAY 6: Anxious Time   11
DAY 7: Making Time in Your Schedule for You   13
DAY 8: Workouts   15
DAY 9: Digesting Thoughts   17
DAY 10: Time at Your Desk   19
DAY 11: Dream Time   21
DAY 12: When Less Is More   23
DAY 13: Chunk Time   25
DAY 14: Digesting Emotions   27
DAY 15: Mealtime   29
DAY 16: Time Earthquakes   31
DAY 17: Doing Nothing   33
DAY 18: Deceleration Time   35
DAY 19: Cutting People Who Suck Your Time   37
DAY 20: Big Life Events   39
DAY 21: Family Time   41
DAY 22: Time to Digest   43
DAY 23: Podcasts and Audiobooks   45

DAY 24: Communication   47

DAY 25: Dealing with To-Do Lists   49

DAY 26: When to Go All Out   51

DAY 27: Eternal Time   53

DAY 28: Time to Catch Your Breath   55

DAY 29: Deathbed Wisdom   57

DAY 30: Gardening   59

DAY 31: Framework before Work   61

DAY 32: Listening to Noise   63

DAY 33: Time on the Ground   65

DAY 34: Smiling   67

DAY 35: Drinking from Infinity   69

DAY 36: Cutting Existing Commitments   71

DAY 37: Workplace Shuffle   73

DAY 38: Daydreaming   74

DAY 39: Time Audit   76

DAY 40: Time and Money   78

DAY 41: Prayer   80

DAY 42: People Have Different Time Stamps   82

DAY 43: Purchase Decisions   84

DAY 44: Chair Time   86

DAY 45: Enjoy This Place   88

DAY 46: Pulling Weeds in Your Life Garden   90

DAY 47: Music   92

DAY 48: Quality Time with Your Family   94

DAY 49: Time and Technology   96

DAY 50: Setting Rituals   98

DAY 51: Stopping Time to Make Love   100

DAY 52: Phone Time   102

DAY 53: Relax the Back of Your Neck   104

DAY 54: Social Media Day Off   106

DAY 55: Five Breaths for You   108

DAY 56: Progressive Relaxation   110

DAY 57: Seasons   113

DAY 58: Reactive Decisions   115

DAY 59: Sweating   117

DAY 60: Time in the Sun   119

DAY 61: Teatime   121

DAY 62: Time by a Fire   123

DAY 63: Time and Light   125

DAY 64: Regular Breaks Daily   127

DAY 65: Shower Time   129

DAY 66: The Rings of a Tree   131

DAY 67: Building a Legacy   133

DAY 68: Time in Bed   135

DAY 69: How Many Heartbeats Do I Have Left?   137

DAY 70: Bath Time   139

DAY 71: Cardio Time   141

DAY 72: Time in the Dark   143

DAY 73: Enlisting Help   145

DAY 74: Time on a Lake   148

DAY 75: Bird-Watching   150

DAY 76: Car Time   152

DAY 77: Time and Weight Gain   154

DAY 78: Time with a Tree   156

DAY 79: Your Bucket List   158

DAY 80: Time to Heal Your Body   160

DAY 81: Vow of Silence   162

DAY 82: Trading Time   164

DAY 83: Time under the Moon   166

DAY 84: Learning Animal Tracks   168
DAY 85: Times with Low Sleep   170
DAY 86: Time to Read   173
DAY 87: Snack Time   174
DAY 88: Time for Your Neighbors   176
DAY 89: Utter Relaxation   178
DAY 90: Turning the Light of Awareness Inward   180
DAY 91: Stretching Out Trapped Time   182
DAY 92: Traumatic Events   185
DAY 93: You'll Be Pushing Up Flowers   187
DAY 94: Time Lost   189
DAY 95: Creative Time   191
DAY 96: Time with the Stars   193
DAY 97: Eye Contact and Face Time   195
DAY 98: Boredom   197
DAY 99: Waiting   199
DAY 100: Time ROI   201

CONCLUSION   203
ACKNOWLEDGMENTS   205
ABOUT THE AUTHOR   209

INTRODUCTION

This is a book about the crazy life we live in which time is always scarce.

We're all struggling to find time in our lives, but somehow there's less of it to go around each year. We're too tired to think, too wired to focus, and less efficient than we want to be. We feel guilty about not getting enough time with our loved ones.

Our perception of the scarcity of time is coupled with the epidemic of stress in the modern world: Stress makes us feel like the walls are closing in on us, which certainly doesn't help us feel better about time. We live in a culture that has lost the script and is absolutely *frantic* about the loss of time.

This concern about time is warranted. Time is the currency of life. We have a certain amount of heartbeats with which to savor life and really taste it. Our time with our families, loved ones, pets, and hobbies is precious, and we cherish it. We also trade our time for money. This money buys us shelter, food, vacations, and college for our kids. We can also squander our money, and it's as though we never had that time at all.

We develop health issues when we're less conscious of time. We then wish we had some time back to make things right. Time is all we have, and it's our most valuable gift in life. When we run out, well, the game is over. We can *look* back, but we can't get it back.

When we don't have a positive connection with the flow of time, we lack purpose. We wander around, aimlessly squandering the time we have, only to regret it later. We get so lost in time that we can't even stop to look at the future and think through the impact of decisions today.

We see this not only on a personal level but also on a societal one: Our biggest political and environmental issues all stem from our personal relationship with time, which is in distress. We can't slow down. We can't stop consuming and polluting.

We all know that we feel starved for time, but what are we actually doing about it? Precious little.

This book is designed to change that and bring us back to a healthier connection with time. By adjusting our relationship with time and finding our center, we can take ownership of our commitments and reprioritize where our valuable time is spent and with whom. In a world where everything is available to us in an endless stream of information and opportunity, the onus is on us to control the gates and take ownership of our time. Our energy, our money, and our time are linked in ways we often don't think about. This book teaches us how in a simple, easy-to-follow, and proven methodology. I've helped thousands of people find more time and peace by becoming Urban Monks.

My goal is to guide you toward what I call time prosperity, which means having the time to accomplish what you desire in life without feeling compressed, stressed, overburdened, or hurried. Time prosperity brings us peace, better decisions, better health, more family time, and a realignment of our priorities in a way that helps us bring fulfillment and purpose back. If you can control your relationship with time and achieve time prosperity, you'll bring down your stress, have more energy, gain more fulfillment, and actually get more done.

So how do we achieve time prosperity? We learn to *stop time*. In this book, I will walk you through ancient spiritual practices and practical life skills that help us stop time by tapping into our innate wisdom, taking control of our calendars, and developing solid boundaries around time commitment. Think of this as the practice of mindful time management.

At the heart of this book, I walk you through a practice called a 100-Day Gong. Based on an ancient Chinese practice, a gong is a designated amount of time that you allot to perform a specific task every day. You pick a particular practice (or set of practices) and designate them as your gong and diligently practice them every day, without fail, for the time period. This not only builds resolve but also forces us to wake up and pay attention to our day-to-day routines. We know that our everyday microhabits lead to the lives we have now. Making small, simple yet significant changes along a longer period of time is the way forward. Change a little here and there and eventually life takes off in wonderful ways. A gong is a powerful way of not only building focus and determination but also ensuring that you train regularly. A gong is a dedicated act of self-love that snaps you out of your daily trance and brings the light of awareness to your consciousness. The more we practice, the more we wake up and the better off we are.

Because it takes at least 90 days for a particular good habit to burn into your nervous system, I have found the 100-Day Gong to be the most appropriate length to practice. You can think of it as a 100-day ritual that helps instill new habits. We all need rituals to snap us out of the trance of modern living and into a deeper personal interface where true change can happen. Instead of asking an already busy person who's on the verge of breaking to *add one more thing* to her chaotic life, we're going to take something you're doing already and provide a swap that will help you liberate more time and energy each day. We're going to check in, relax a bit, and slightly alter a current habit by offering up a better way. We do this each day and slowly build better routines.

Some practices will stick, and others will not. That's fine. The key is to slowly and gently unlock more time and therefore more energy and enthusiasm in your life through the practice. You'll keep some of the efficiencies or maybe come back to some later in life, but taking a 100-day walk through your life will fundamentally transform your relationship with time, energy, money, people, and life itself.

With short chapters, each day offers a quick lesson and action plan. That's it. Some of the lessons focus on specific activities that you probably wish you had time to do. Some focus on general ways to find more time for however you want to use it. Some may be easy for you, and others may rattle your core. Over 100 days, life will be different. *You* will be different, and your relationship with time (and therefore life) will be fundamentally transformed for the better.

The ideal way to use this book is to run through it from start to finish over the next 100 days (yes, that means start now!) and simply do each day's practice. As you roll forward, you'll find that certain things have come along on the ride with you. You may have huge realizations one day and fundamentally change the way you do a certain thing. Other days, you may go through a practice and not connect with it deeply. That's cool. Roll forward day by day and see what habits you pick up along the way. Write your notes all over this book. Journal in it and circle things. This work is *your* process. It's your innate wisdom that's being tapped as we go. Document it.

Once you've finished your first 100 days, I recommend using this book randomly each day. Let's call it gong roulette. Carry the book around with you and randomly open to any chapter and make that your day's gong. You'll have seen that practice at least once in your first pass, and now you'll have a chance to revisit it. You're never going to be the same person when you come back to a chapter, so you'll learn much about your journey as a human on this planet as you go.

Now go live your life and practice it. Let's get to work. We've got 100 days together, starting today!

DAY 1

assembling your life garden

Today we look at life through the filter of a natural metaphor. Imagine your life is a garden. You have limited water and need to leave space for each plant to flourish. Some may be bigger and more important to you than others. Some you may not even like but are obliged to keep there.

Think about what's important to you. What would make it into your Life Garden? Family? Career? Health? Relationships? Music? What's important in your life?

List these items and then imagine how much energy needs to go into the sustained growth of each. Think of your energy as the water you need to nourish and grow each plant. It comes in the currency of time, effort, willpower, and attention. If you were to adequately nourish each plant, what would it take?

Some may require far more time and energy than others. Make an allowance for that. New cars cost money. If you want one, you'll have to either make more (which means more water in the career area) or take away some funds from your family or elsewhere. Take a cold, hard look at what you *say you value* and then reconcile that against how much water (time, energy, attention, money, focus) you have to keep that plant happy and healthy. Can you manage to keep certain plants alive while directing the flow of your water to certain others for the time being?

Get realistic about how many plants you need to water and

cultivate. You have room for five to ten plants and that's it. Guard against any new ones that may be introduced into your garden, and pull up the ones that are sucking valuable resources away from your most important plants. Consider these weeds. It takes focus and dedication, but this is critically important. By saying yes to something new, you're effectively saying no to your existing plants. You'll find yourself watering newcomer weeds and diverting away from the plants you've deemed important in your life. Does this sound familiar?

This practice will help you grow more mindful. It's important to set a Life Garden and then use it as a filter to see if new plants can root. Does something fall within the domain of an existing plant? If so, how much water will it pull from the others? Can you afford the shift? Is it a completely new plant? Where will you draw the water from to make room for it? Is that the best use of your resources? Be honest.

Qigong means energy work (qi = energy and gong = work). It is the cultivation of one's personal energy through a yogic practice. The actual term "gong" is used to describe our practice here.

Over time, with qigong and meditation, you'll have access to more energy, personal power, and clarity. This'll help you draw upon more water for existing plants or newcomers. But for now assume your water (energy, time, and focus) is limited to what it currently is. With that, how do you need to allocate this water to make each plant flourish? Let's get clear on where you want it to go and then assess if that's what's happening. If not, let's make adjustments.

Using the Life Garden metaphor can help you be honest about how much time and energy you have to commit to things. This way you don't overcommit, and you also simultaneously avoid the stress and regret that come with not getting things done.

When we align our goals with our plans, we plug in our focus and willpower to make it work.

DAY 2

time for gratitude

Today we pull over and take some time to be grateful for what we have. Gratitude is good medicine and is always time well spent. It helps relieve stress and build positive energy, and it gives us great perspective on life.

When's the last time you did this? Are you hardwired to be grateful, or is it something you have to remind yourself about? Practicing gratitude is healthy. It helps paint a worldview of optimism and hope. People who practice it are consistently happier—we've seen this in multiple studies.

What tends to happen with people who are depressed and stuck is a phenomenon called stacking. This is when something bad happens to us and we take that isolated event and attach it to a series of other "bad" isolated events and create a pessimistic narrative.

Let's say you stub your toe and drop your phone. People who stack go to a place where "this always happens to me; I have such bad luck; I remember when I tripped in college and was embarrassed" and on and on. A bill could come in and remind you of all of your financial woes, or something as trivial as your favorite team losing could trigger your personal narrative of how you married the wrong person.

It doesn't make sense, but it's what we tend to do. It's a downward spiral that drags us into a "my life sucks" narrative that doesn't serve us. It also makes us less fun to be around.

Gratitude is a wonderful antidote for this tendency. Today let's practice this. Grab a piece of paper or pick up your phone and simply start making a list of all the things you're grateful for. It could be your kids, your cat, your accomplishments, a tasty lunch you had recently, or the clouds in the sky. Just keep writing.

Spend at least 10 minutes going through this exercise and don't stop. Even if it sounds stupid, write it down and keep flowing down your list. It may take a second to recall some of these items. That's fine. The act of recalling them delivers a powerful therapeutic and spiritual value.

Once you're finished with your list, stop and ask yourself how you feel. How did you feel before you started, and how do you feel after? Any difference? Take note of it.

As you go through your day, keep your list with you. Take a look at it a few more times and do a quick read through. Stop on any item that grabs your attention and let that gratitude fill your heart. Sit with the *feeling* of gratitude toward whatever the given item is. Bask in its sunshine, and let it fill you.

At the end of today go back and recall how you felt in the morning and how you feel on the other side. Any difference? Chances are, it'll be subtle but definitely there. If you like what this is doing, keep your list with you tomorrow and add to it. In fact, see about adding things as they come up for you, and make this list a growing scroll of things you're grateful for. The more you do it, the better it'll serve you. Over time, this practice will radically transform your life and change your mood toward all things. It takes away the friction and allows us to live in a healthier, timeless space.

DAY 3

nature

Today's lesson is simple: Step outside and learn from the ultimate teacher. Nature is our guiding light when it comes to cycles and rhythms. She functions under a perfect ebb and flow of counterbalancing principles. Heat and cold balance with light and dark. Growth and decay are fully realized in cycles of the year, as are birth and death. Nature has all the wisdom you need, packed into plain sight.

We've simply forgotten to look.

Today's practice is to step outside and spend some quiet time in nature. Even if a public park or back lawn of an office park is all you can access, I am positive that there is going to be some semblance of the natural world available to you today if you open your eyes and look for it. Go there.

Sit in a comfortable spot and start to breathe deeply to your lower abdomen. Relax into your breathing and sink into the sounds all around you. Feel the wind on your face and maybe take off your shoes and wiggle your toes into the dirt. If you have the luxury to fully immerse, get into some clay or bury your body at the beach. Break down the wall and allow for nature's majesty to touch you and surround your senses.

Trees can get to hundreds of years in age, but the pebbles below your feet are millions of years old. Where did they come from? Were they part of some large rock aeons ago? How did they get here?

Now observe the dirt under your feet. Long ago, certain fungal elements evolved to break down rock and create dirt. With the coming of bacteria, *Protozoa*, nematodes, and multiple other life-forms, the dirt started to become soil. This allowed for certain life-forms to take inorganic materials and make them available to the plant kingdom, which then took off and spread across the planet. Those plants adapted to drink light and create energy from the sun, trapping energy in carbohydrate bonds. This became the fuel for certain animals to eat, and fast-forward several million years, here you are.

The microscopic life under your feet created a long cascade of processes that eventually allowed you to be here as a consumer of sunlight via plants. If you eat animals, you're capturing the sunlight they ingested via the plants they consumed.

Life: It's all around you. You're breathing it in right now as you're reading this. Millions of bacteria and viruses just entered your lungs and are all over your skin. They help you interact with the natural world all around you. They help defend against invaders. They are part of the ecosystem of your body, which is part of the ecosystem of the planet. This is all going on while you go through your day, millions upon millions of life-forms living their lives, oblivious to your bills or petty dramas.

Sit outside in the symphony of nature and notice the oddity of scale. On the one hand, you're this universe of life with bugs in you and on your skin, all interacting as an ecosystem. On the other, you're a tiny speck on a single planet at the edge of a regular galaxy that is light-years from the next.

Up and down it's all amazing, and *you* sit in the middle of all of it. You are a focal point where infinity collides into a single point of time and space. How can you make sense of it all? The only way is to open your heart and fall into the wonder that it induces. This way, we don't take ourselves so seriously. It helps us think about the big questions and puts in perspective where we stand in the grand scheme of things.

You only get a moment of time here as the person you think you are. What are you going to do with it?

DAY 4

e-mail time

E-mail has become an integral part of our lives. It became a powerful way of communicating, which quickly became the new norm for businesses all over the world. E-mail is great. You can attach files, pictures, and videos efficiently. You get people what they need and move on with your life.

So what's the problem? Volume. We've become slaves to the inventions that were created to make life easier. Now we're drowning in e-mails. Every store, car dealer, app company, and vitamin peddler is sending you e-mails almost daily. Spam has become an enormous issue that we all deal with, and it doesn't seem to be going away.

Today we deal with this. It doesn't make sense to look at your e-mail every time your phone or computer chimes. It distracts you from the task at hand and keeps you unfocused. What other people want you to look at isn't going to get you through your day efficiently. In fact, every time you look away, you lose momentum and clarity in what you were doing.

Let's set up some chunk time for you to check e-mail. Depending on the volume you deal with, set 30 to 60 minutes for e-mail in the late morning and another block toward the late afternoon. This is your dedicated e-mail time. The key is to get in, handle it, and get out. One way to do this is to run through all the messages in the morning block, handle anything that can be responded to in the first 5 minutes, star the important ones you need to get back to, and delete or mark as spam all the others. You'll have another block later in the day to get to the longer ones if need be.

On that note, you need a good spam filter so the junk doesn't even get put in your face. There are a number of good ways to do this, and you'll have to find one that suits your unique needs. Make a habit of marking items you didn't elect to receive as spam within your e-mail program. This teaches the software what not to send you and helps you keep your inbox clean. With spam out of your face, look at the key communications that deserve your time and start to back your way out of long e-mail chains that waste it.

The secret to e-mail chunk time is to book it on your calendar, communicate clearly (so you needn't go back and forth), and clear your plate. This way it doesn't sit on your mind and pester you; it also doesn't languish unread or half-answered. The sweeter result of this play is increased focus and concentration on the work you're doing. If you're working on a document, stay in it. Spreadsheet? Cool, get your work done there. Driving? Well, what were you thinking checking your phone anyhow?

The goal is to maintain clarity in your work and handle e-mail at designated times. Rearrange your schedule to chunk your e-mail time, and make this your plan for the day. Try to do it again tomorrow, then the next day. In a few weeks, you'll see the clutter dissipate and your life get better. Stick with this, and pay close attention to holding the line. Some discipline will pay off here. People may push back. That's fine. Deliver everything that's required of you and get your job done. Efficiency is key. Once people learn to sync to your new rhythm, the difference in productivity and sanity will emanate from your vicinity. The key is to get better at what you do by curating your day to serve you and free up your time.

DAY 5

when to lie low

There's a time to jam and a time to chill. A wise person can know where she stands and adjust her speed accordingly. We all have deadlines and eras in life when time is tight and compressed; if we know how to protect ourselves during these times, they can be filled with energy, excitement, and momentum. But we can't stay in hyperdrive for long, and if we don't learn how to turn it off, we can get burned out or burned up. That's how our economy is set up— the constant grind. If you can work your way off that hamster wheel, you'll find yourself in a much healthier position in life.

If you're stuck in such a lifestyle, it is prudent to understand the ebb and flow of these rhythms and adjust your own velocity manually. This means knowing when to slow way down. You still may need to go through certain motions, but this lesson is about learning to identify the moments when you need to be redlining and the moments when you can—and should—intentionally take your foot off the gas.

Today let's examine the bigger cycles of your busy life. Are you in a "push hard and get there" phase, or are you between deadlines? Are you required to leave it all on the court right now, or can you ease off the gas and replenish your reserves? Only you can determine this.

One thing to take into account is your current energy level. On a scale of 1 to 10 (10 being the highest energy), how much do you have right now? A score of 1 means you can hardly get out of bed and are totally depleted, and a 6 means you're doing okay but certainly not feeling great. What's your honest answer to this?

Now here's the kicker: If you were to factor your willpower out of the equation, then what would your number be? You see, most of us are forcing energy out to keep up with the demands of our lives. We use our willpower to keep us in overdrive so we can get through, and our bodies, our minds, and our relationships are paying the price. What's your honest number if you factor out willpower?

Now take that number and think about what you need to do for yourself to bring it up and feel better. When can you slow down? How would you do it?

Today take 30 minutes and simply only do what you *feel like doing.* This may turn into a nap, since most of us are usually exhausted. That's fine. It's a step in the right direction, which honors the spirit of today's gong. From there, tonight start to think about what else you think would help bring balance to your life.

Can you take a week in the backcountry? Maybe you can factor in a day off now and again to go to the spa and catch your breath. Perhaps you need to learn to meditate and at least slow your roll on your daily burn. Each life is different, and we all need our own medicine to come to balance. What would your medicine be?

Now that you've taken an honest look at your energy levels and thought about what you may need to bounce back, look at your calendar and book some downtime for yourself. Make it a date, a trip, a sabbatical, or whatever it needs to be. Book it, and honor it. You'll need the energy to get through your life with your health and sanity intact.

When can you pull over and take a breather? Book it in your calendar today.

DAY 6

anxious time

The way the modern world is stacked up, unfortunately, we get a lot of anxious time. This is time spent in anticipation, frustration, aggravation, and, well, you know.

So how can we leverage this time to become our teacher? There's information packed into our internal state and how it is cooking at these moments, so why not leverage it for growth?

The velocity of time is oftentimes too fast when we're anxious. The blood flow is going to the hindbrain, which is telling us to fight, flee, or panic. It is being cut off from our internal organs, immunity, digestion, and higher reasoning. Again, sadly, we run a lot of miles in this lane, so let's take this as an opportunity for greater awareness.

Scan your mind today at random times and ask yourself if you sense anxiety. Make that your mantra for the day. Keep scanning and checking in to see how you feel. When you identify a state that you would label as anxious, the game is on. Now, it could feel like "slightly anxious" or "agitated" and that's good enough for our exercise today. The key is to grab some sample data from this state to reflect on.

Okay so you've identified an anxious state. Now what?

Ask yourself the next series of questions:

- What does this feel like?
- Is it warm or cold?
- Where do I feel it in my body?
- Is it moving around?

- Can I attribute a quality to this feeling? For example, is it dull, fuzzy, heavy, or painful?

And then follow with the next series of questions:

- Where did this feeling come from?
- Was there a thought or a conversation that elicited it?
- When did it start?
- Do I often feel this when thinking about this same situation?
- How is this serving me?

The next step is to acknowledge the way you're feeling and then take 10 deep breaths to your lower abdomen. Put a smile on your face and stretch your body out however you need. Did any of it shift? Now how do you feel?

The challenge of today's exercise is to isolate a moment when you're feeling anxious and use it as feedback for the way you experience time and life in those moments. The more awareness you can bring to this experience, the better you'll get at moving out of that feeling and, later on, the better you'll be at avoiding the reactions that lead to that state in the first place.

DAY 7

making time in your schedule for you

Today's lesson is simple. Make a list of all the things you want to do for yourself. This should include exercise, personal time, family time, reading, yoga, massage, or whatever else you keep telling yourself you want to do. Jot down these items.

Take a look at this list and see if it's complete. Make sure it reflects your desires for self-care. If you did these things, would you feel complete in life? Would you be rested, calm, fit, and happier? What else would need to be there in order to feel that way? Write it down. Next, sort these items into the order of importance you'd put them in. The most critical one should go on top and then down from there.

Now let's do a quick reality check. Let's open your calendar. Look at your schedule this week (or any average week if you're doing something vastly different right now). What's on your schedule? How many of the items on your list are actually reflected on your calendar? Is there a block of time set aside for you to get to the gym? How about family time? Have you scheduled time to read? Where do these things fall on your timeline?

If you're like most people, practically none of your self-care items shows up on your calendar. That says something to the universe and your inner self—namely, that you don't prioritize these things.

Here's the rule: If it's important enough to you and your life, then it should be on your calendar.

Look at what happens to your time. The world will always serve up items, tasks, events, calls, meetings, or drama to fill your time. *Nature hates a vacuum.* Your schedule will get gobbled up by the chaos all around you unless you step in and own it.

You have to hold the line for those things you consider important.

Today go through your list and knock something off of your calendar until there is room for one of your top items. How can you start to incorporate the items on your list into your calendar so you *make the time* to take care of yourself? Where can you slip in a workout, a phone call, some personal time in order to feel whole? The key is managing your burn rate. If you put all the self-care off until next weekend or that next vacation, well, you see where that has gotten you. So how do you live a balanced life *each day* that helps move you ahead and serve your long-term happiness? You build it in.

Go through and build your important items into your calendar today. It may take some creative positioning or even some delayed starts, since this next week or so may already be jammed. That's okay. Just book it. Commit in a way that you can't back out of, whether that's putting money down, going with a friend, or writing it down in pen. Once it's in there, it'll start to bring sanity to your life. Don't overdo it and neglect your work, but strike a balance that you can keep up with.

The key lesson in this exercise is to think through your needs and build them into your day. However, *none of this will work unless you honor those blocks.* It's easy to see a workout block and book something over it when you can't find time. Push things back on the calendar. Most things can wait. Maybe build some open-time slots for stuff that comes up in order to make room for chaos and spontaneous guest arrivals. This is a process for you to practice and eventually master. Honor your appointments with yourself and you'll reap the rewards. Hold the line and you'll start to feel full again.

DAY 8

workouts

Let's take a look at your exercise habits today. There are lots of changes in our understanding of exercise that have come about in the past few years. The most important one in relation to your time is that you needn't work out for an hour per day, five days per week to get the best results.

High-intensity interval training (HIIT) is where it's at now. That means getting to your maximum heart rate, panting and recovering, and then going back up.

Your practice today is to go to the park and find an open field. Warm up for 5 minutes and stretch your hips, hamstrings, ankles, and torso. When ready, sprint across the field at half of your top speed to the other side. When there, do 10 to 25 pushups (depending on your fitness level). Then sprint back to the original side at three-quarters of your full speed and do 50 jumping jacks. Take 2 minutes to recover, repeat the sequence a few times, and then go home. All in all, your entire workout can last 15 minutes today.

This type of workout pushes your body beyond its current physiological comfort zone, which triggers hormesis, a metabolic state that expresses genes that help us grow in the right way. This kind of exercise will help spawn new mitochondria and beef up existing ones. These are the powerhouses of our cells, and more mitochondria equal more energy available to us.

Working out in intense spurts may take a while to get used to. Make sure you stretch for a few minutes, and stop if you experience any joint pain. In fact, it's always better to work with a trainer who can monitor you and keep you on the right side of the health line. Be safe.

The moral of the story here is this: You needn't log in the time doing the same routine on the treadmill day in and day out. In fact, once you've hit a level where the body gets comfortable, you're not getting results anymore. That means you need to push yourself.

Go for intense spurts of activity to challenge your heart and your muscles, and then recover fully. This will not only give you better results in your workouts but also free up some time each day that you had (hopefully already) allocated toward exercise.

Getting out of the "clock-in, clock-out" mentality of working out is an important quantum leap you can make in your life. It isn't the quantity of time but the *quality*. How focused are you on your workout? Can you breathe into and slow down that bicep curl? If so, then a few solid reps do the trick, and you can move on and live your life.

Your time is precious. If you build a culture of moving around all day, your resting metabolic rate doesn't dip. If you avoid sitting and stretch periodically, you get less stagnant. This allows you to then get an efficient workout. You get better results in less time. Great! Now go take a nap, make love, or read a book with your newly absorbed time. Better yet, sit on a cushion and contemplate the eternal nature of your life force. Then you'll truly be free.

DAY 9

digesting thoughts

Have you ever suffered from thought indigestion? This is when some information comes across that needs thought and analysis. Maybe you have a complicated work campaign on your mind, or maybe you're contemplating a sticky divorce with lots of fallout and challenges. Some things we simply need to spend time thinking about. This is natural and appropriate, like avoiding swimming after a meal so you can digest. We all try to make space for that, but what about mental digestion?

When people have a backlog of mental processing that needs to happen, it creates stress. You have stuff on your mind, yet life keeps coming at you. You're not present with your family, you seem distant in conversations, or you space out and miss your exit. Why? Because you're working through information, ruminating and assimilating. It is normal to do this—healthy, in fact—but *not* while doing certain things. Distracted driving isn't safe. Being distant and unavailable for your kids leads to many challenges. It is like being stuck in another time while stumbling through the present.

So how do we fix this? We allot time for digestion. You have to honor the fact that it can take some time to process certain information. Exercise and hiking are great places to do some of this. They get the body moving so you can integrate your thoughts and process them in a healthy way. That's why a lot of people find sanity in working out: They use the time to process amassed thoughts.

Think about where you get to do this in your life. Do you have a healthy outlet for thought digestion, or are you guilty of not being present with the people in your life? Where can you move things around to make time for this?

You need to do it.

It'll drive better decisions and help to dramatically alleviate stress levels.

When we eat food, we need to break it down and assimilate it. Lots of modern problems have emerged because people don't chew and instead eat too fast. Today think about how you may be doing this with thoughts. What would your life look like without the mental backlog you drag around all day?

DAY 10

time at your desk

Whomen's the last time you did an audit of how much you sit? Is it all day minus a lunchtime walk? Did you factor in your drive time? How about the hour on the sofa, watching your show?

Take a few minutes to calculate your average time sitting today. The number may be staggering.

You are not alone. Sitting is considered the new smoking, and there are multiple studies that show how terrible it is for our health. In fact, a study in the *American Journal of Epidemiology* ties stagnant lifestyle with a greater risk of mortality in both men and women.

How does this relate to time? It is a central anchor to where we lose time.

The more you sit, the more you stagnate. Your circulation diminishes, and your metabolic rate drops. In fact, anything over 30 minutes at a time shows a slowdown of flow in the body. This means fewer calories burned at rest, less lymph drainage to help detoxify, less energy output from our mitochondria, and, frankly, less life force to work with. Our light starts to dim and flicker when we sit too long.

This directly robs us of time and degrades the *quality of the time* we experience.

How?

It brings down our energy levels so we are less clear and focused at work. This means getting less done and having more on our minds.

It may mean less money earned so more time needs to go into longer hours to cover the gap. Less money usually equals more stress, which degrades quality of life.

If we have less energy, then we don't feel like moving around or exercising. That spirals down into more weight gain and inertia. Then we spend our precious time feeling guilty about not exercising and depressed that we don't feel like it right now.

We put things off because we lack the energy and enthusiasm. Those things stay on our mind and haunt us when we go home. When we greet our families, we're not all there mentally because we're tired, still have work on our minds, and are trying to figure out when we could sneak away to exercise.

That seldom happens, so we get stuck in that inner dialogue of "Nothing is working in my life," which pulls us out of the present moment. We then miss a cue that our daughter is having trouble with her friends at school and feel like a loser parent. It goes on and on.

You see, how we do one thing affects how we do everything. Today you are going to take this back. Stand when you're on the phone rather than staying seated. Get some boxes and build a standing desk. If you can't do that, set a timer and stand up every 25 minutes. Move around, stretch, take some deep breaths, get some water, and then go back. Take a walk after lunch, and make phone calls on your cell phone so you can pace around.

Do not allow your body to settle into the dreary sleep of corporate demise. Today you keep your body awake, which will, in turn, energize your mind. This will roll forward into all aspects of your life, and you'll quickly see the benefits downstream.

Still water breeds poison. Get up and keep moving.

DAY 11

dream time

Positive growth means reaching back into the gunk of the past and healing it so it doesn't infect our present. This is where most people are stuck. They can't be in the *now* since they're trapped in the *past*, lugging it around, feeling crappy.

I'm not saying that dealing with this stuff is either fun or easy, *but it is the only game in town.* You have to become whole if you want to be a fully embodied human. Dreams can help you with this.

Carl Jung was one of the godfathers of modern psychology. He wrote prolifically about the dream state and how it is our link to the collective unconscious. This is where we tap into the juicy stuff. It is where much of our psycho-emotional baggage gets left to fester. If we don't look at this stuff, like a field of weeds, it begins to grow out of control. We eventually start to say things that are nasty. We do things we may regret. The ugly stuff starts to rear its face, and we don't know what's come over us. It starts to overflow, *and it isn't pretty.*

We have a profound connection with the unconscious and subconscious realms through our dream state. Stuff comes up that can help us see patterns in our life. We can see beyond the facades that our ego constructs and dig deeply into the emotional baggage that hinders us. This baggage happened in some past time and got trapped in our energy fields. It haunts us and holds us back.

Today spend a few minutes trying to remember some recent dreams. Work to remember. It's normal if you don't, but you may be surprised what's in there. After this exercise, grab a notebook and place it by your bed. Tell yourself that the *first thing* you'll do tomorrow morning is to write down your dreams. The closer to waking the better, as you'll find how quickly the memories fade into obscurity. Your dream journal is something that can become a powerful catalyst for change in your life. If you couple it with a normal day journal, you can go back and look at the connection between what was going on in your life and the dreams you had around the same time. There is often much wisdom, symbolic imagery, subtle clues, and notable omens that slip through the dream state for us. Look to become more aware of this thread, and use it as an oracle or guiding light in your daily life.

The better you get at pulling back some of these dreams and putting them to paper, the more amazing lessons you can call upon from the other side. There's a wealth of information you can access that'll help you heal your past and stop carrying it into the present. Dreams are the conduit.

DAY 12

when less is more

Today let's look at the more-is-better culture that's infected our consciousness. It is everywhere. We've become good at manufacturing things and have taken off with a global economy based on consumption. In fact, we're known as consumers more than anything to the businesses we deal with.

How empowering is that? Is your life more meaningful than your ability to produce and consume for the economy? It certainly is.

Let's take a look at how much stuff you have today. Walk through your house. Don't forget the garage, attic, extra rooms, and storage facilities off-site. Run through and build a mental tab of how much stuff you've accumulated over the years. Is it still serving you, or is it weighing you down?

How many of these items have you not used (or even looked at) in over a year? When do you plan on looking at them again? We often hang on to items thinking they're too valuable to let go of, only to eventually chuck them years later. Can you identify any of these items today? If you're thinking of keeping these items for your kids, maybe ask them if they'd even want such a thing.

The problem with stuff is that it weighs you down. Whether you know it consciously or not, there's a part of your consciousness that has to hold space for the things you keep in life.

Today let's look at where you've gone outside of yourself to buy comfort. Take whatever you're not using and get rid of it. Simplify and clear your space. This helps clear your mind and free up your consciousness. Inside that reality is more time and happiness.

What can you get rid of today? Donating items is wonderful and can help people in need. Can you allow for this with certain items in your life? Which ones? Don't put them aside into another pile that's never going to leave your house: Gather them together today, and get them out now.

Which items are simply trash? Now is the day to trash them, even if you feel guilty that you never got around to learning how to use that ice cream maker that's now broken or that your kid never uses his hockey stick anymore. Learn your lesson here. Landfills are vomiting up the things we thought we needed. What can you learn about what not to buy from this exercise?

Clearing physical space has the added bonus of clearing mental space. This is liberating for the mind. It gives us the spaciousness we've been looking for. The challenge has always been our orientation. We've been trained to look *outward* for solutions: "What kind of shoes, makeup, truck, exercise gear, or crystal can I buy to make me whole and happy?" By now you should know that this doesn't work. Happiness and peace come from within. They come from simplicity.

Less is more in this scenario.

Get rid of the junk, and make a habit of questioning whether you really need a certain item before purchasing it. You can't buy comfort and peace, but you can breathe to that place.

DAY 13

chunk time

One of the most powerful ways of leveraging time and feeling in control of your schedule is learning how to chunk time. This means assigning segments of time on your calendar for specific activities and keeping to those. E-mail time is for checking and writing e-mail. Family time is just that—no other distractions then. If you're working on a report, that's all you do, and if you're on a date, be there with her.

The key to getting this is to let go of the false notion that multitasking somehow makes us better. It doesn't work. It makes us more distracted, fragmented, and anxious. The most effective people do one thing at a time; they stay focused, get it done, and then move on to the next thing. That next thing could be taking a nap, and guess what? They do that well, too. Why? Because when you've committed to one thing at a time, you can then shut out all other tasks or distractions and stay focused. Knowing that you've scheduled the important stuff for the day means you don't have to worry about running out of time. When you get to your allotted nap time, you can then rest deeply and sink into the best sleep of your life.

Today have a look at how you run your schedule. Are you trying to do too many things at once? Are you overcommitted throughout the day and find yourself struggling to plug up holes in a sinking ship? That's common. Time scarcity goes hand in hand with attention scarcity. If your focus is fragmented, you can't do anything well;

you'll likely find yourself getting stressed out as new items come up when old ones are still incomplete.

Think of your daily schedule like a computer. How many applications do you have open? If you're working on a document, does it help to open your e-mail, texts, accounting, weather apps, and a video game all at once? Of course not! We all see how the performance of our system is diminished that way, yet we're willing to live like that ourselves.

Today organize your activities into chunks of time for the things you have to do in your life. Lunchtime is for eating and recovery. Work is best done when you're focused on one task at a time. Engaging with children requires you to be there—no sense in splintering your presence, as they'll notice and nag you anyway. Commit to staying focused on items at their allotted times and see what happens. You'll have to curate your calendar to fit the new framework you create, and most important, you'll need to stick to it. Hold the line or you're lost.

Make sure you schedule chunks of time for rest, recovery, food, family, and fun; if you only schedule work and obligations, something will break. We need dynamic balance in our lives, and adhering to a healthy schedule allows us to have that. Once you get the hang of this, you'll find yourself more relaxed and happy. There's a spaciousness in knowing that you're doing exactly what you need to be doing right now. It's all the other crap crowding into your present timeline that creates the stress. One thing at a time will get you there faster and give you plenty more time to enjoy the ride.

DAY 14

digesting emotions

igesting thoughts is important, but what about emotions? These are the bites we often choke on. When someone says something that upsets you, how easy is it to move on? How long before you're finished?

For most of us, that takes a while. Part of the training of an urban monk is to learn to build a positive-energy bank account and be able to allow things to roll right off you. That doesn't mean certain things don't impact you. It's human. Say your kid is doing poorly in school. That sucks. Parents die. So do pets. Tragedies happen all around the world. These things *should* make us angry, sad, frustrated, and upset. Again, that's human.

The problem lies *in denial*. Do you give yourself enough time to grieve a loss? Do you allow yourself the luxury of getting angry for 5 minutes and then cooling off? Most of us don't, especially when it comes to anger. We judge it. We are ashamed to express it, so we hide it. That way it slowly festers and builds into a shitty mood or passive-aggressive attitude. Stress has a similar effect. It bounces around in our system until some unsuspecting person takes a full-frontal assault from us that she probably doesn't deserve.

Sound familiar?

This is a big issue in our culture and where most people are stuck in the past. How often do you go back to a moment when someone said something that bothered you? How viscerally do you relive the experience? How attached are you to *that time*? The answer is usually very much so.

Emotional indigestion puts a time lag on our existence and keeps us vibrating in the past. The "should've, would've, could've" scenarios play in our brains, and we are stuck *then* and not fully *here now*.

Today think about when this has happened in your life. Maybe it's happening right now. Are you dragging something around today from last night? Last year? There's a good chance.

Step one is to acknowledge that you're there. See it. Feel it.

Now go back to the event and fill your heart with love. Breathe white light into it on the inhale and have that light disperse throughout your entire body on the exhale. Put a smile on your face and allow your heart to soften with this practice.

Next forgive those involved and bring light and healing to the scenario you've chosen to look at. This may take a couple of minutes, but let it happen; it'll be time well spent versus the countless moments lost over the next several week and years.

Every time you get a chance today, recall that particular harsh event and continue the practice of filling your heart with white light and then bringing love and forgiveness to the memory you've chosen to heal. Make this today's gong. Commit to healing it, and fill your heart with enough love and energy to make it happen.

DAY 15

mealtime

Today we focus on our meals. It's so easy to get carried away in our busy lives and forget to slow down around food. Eating has been lost in the frenzy of activities and has been relegated to another box to check on our daily list. Not today.

Let's take it back.

Mealtime is ritual time. It is our opportunity to pause and embrace a slower quality of time so we can nourish our bodies, absorb nutrients, and relax into the digestive process. This is where we get strong.

Our fight-or-flight sympathetic nervous system is in overdrive. This is where our body is in crisis mode. Stress signals our body to store fat, move blood to reactive parts of the brain, tense muscles, and draw energy away from digestion and immunity. That's not a good way to roll long-term, but that's where many of us live. It is time to break this cycle.

Today every time you sit down for a meal, take 10 breaths down to your lower abdomen and relax into your body. This immediately settles you into a different state. The parasympathetic nervous system is where we digest, recover, heal, and relax. Lower abdominal breathing naturally puts us there.

Drop in and settle your breath.

Now let's look at your meal. This food is actually *life*. If you're eating right, you should draw all of your food from unprocessed sources. This means real vegetables, fruits, grains, or meats (if you so choose). All of this food came from things that were recently alive. You are ingesting this life and allowing it to power your body and nourish your cells. This life has lain down on a sacrificial altar and is allowing you to continue living. That's heavy.

Take a moment and give thanks for the food in front of you. Look at it for a minute. Smell it for 20 seconds. Take time to taste, and chew it at least 20 times before swallowing. After each bite, put down your utensil (or the food itself, if you're eating with your hands) while you chew and swallow. Slow down and adopt an attitude of thankfulness and reverence for food, and it'll transform your entire life.

You not only will be more relaxed but also will eat less, chew more, digest better, assimilate and nourish your cells, and have less inflammation in your body. There are so many good things that happen around this ritual that you will be shocked to see the benefits. They accumulate over time.

Today is the first day of the rest of your life. Take time with each meal today and savor it. Slow down and enjoy the ritual of eating. It may take 10 extra minutes to eat, but you'll be less tired, less wired, and more energized after the meal.

Ideally, take 10 to 15 minutes after eating to simply relax and enjoy some downtime. Making this a habit will give you more energy, clarity, and overall health to run the rest of your day effectively.

DAY 16

time earthquakes

Can you remember the last event that knocked you off your time tracks? This is something that jolted you off a day's timeline and made you stop and think. It could have been an accident, an illness, a business challenge, or a lover. Something happens to interrupt our pattern and pushes us off of our existing flow of time. Something diverts our timeline. It can slow down or speed up depending on the nature of the event, but the notable piece is that time takes on a different quality right after this event. This distortion may last a few hours for several years, depending on how much it bent and folded your reality. It can feel like an earthquake that shook your entire foundation.

The lesson in this is twofold. First off, what can you do differently the next time? Were you caught unprepared and couldn't get out of your pjs for a week? How did that serve you? We can learn from past occurrences so as to avoid mistakes the next time. Hindsight is 20/20, but we only get it when we look back and learn from the past.

The second lesson is far subtler. If this external event was able to shift the quality or velocity of time, then why can't you do it on your own? We often accept when big life events, trauma, or bad news shifts our perception of time, but how is that normal? If it can happen in one of those events, it means it can happen *period*. So let's peel back that fact and help you learn to make it happen on your own terms in life.

Stopping time happens within our own consciousness. We can control our perception of the flow of the space-time continuum by elevating our consciousness to a higher level. This is where the perception of the ancients was able to be so expansive. This is why meditation and yoga have lasted so long and continue to serve us. We can actually hold the dial on the velocity of time once we understand how to adjust our internal state. So let's do this.

There's a particular practice I'm going to teach you today that'll help you feel the flux in time velocity. It is called the Time Dilation Qigong Practice.

You can view it here: http://theurbanmonk.com/resources/ch2/

Watch the video and do the work. It'll take no more than 15 minutes, but with some practice, you should start to sense a difference in the quality of time as you perceive it. Look for the in-between moments, when there's a slightly different vibe going from fast to slow and back. The more you stretch your perception of these moments, the more you'll understand about the veil of time and how to navigate it. Some things are better left unsaid.

Do the practice and see for yourself.

DAY 17

doing nothing

One of the central tenets of Taoism is called *wu wei,* which is a state of "not doing." This may sound foreign to our Western minds, but if you think about it, it's good medicine for us. We live in a culture of emphasized action. We're only as good as our productive capacity, and we're driven to perform and stay busy far too often. Our world is crazy.

So how do we bring balance to this? Practice *being* today. It may take a while to get the hang of it, and you may think you're going crazy, but that's just the monkey mind talking. Take 10 minutes to simply sit through the discomfort and be.

How do we do this? Easy: Just don't do anything.

Now what? Keep not doing anything.

How do I do that?

Aha.

Therein lies the problem. We still try to "do" not doing. Does that make sense? Of course not, but most of us know no other way. We are a culture of doers. Our activity defines us and drives us to better ourselves. Maybe it's just momentum or our parents talking, but whatever it is, notice the tendency toward perpetual motion in your life.

Watch how your mind is always looking for something to do, and even when you practice nonaction, you can catch it doing something. You may be planning dinner, thinking about what Shelly said, moving your attention to the itch on your nose, or complaining to yourself that this exercise isn't working: That's all activity.

Okay, so let's take an intermediary step on your path to nonaction training. Today when practicing this exercise (10 minutes or more would be ideal), you can have one thing you're allowed to do. You can ask yourself *one question*, and you can do this over and over. It is the only thing you should do during the whole exercise.

What's the question? Ask yourself, "What am I doing right now?" and whatever the answer is, stop doing that and *relax*.

Next ask it again: "What am I doing right now?" And again, relax.

It takes Zen monks years to master this, but if you commit and do the exercise without all the excuses that come to mind, you may get a glimpse of the other side.

What other side? The peaceful serenity of a relaxed mind. Imagine what it could be like if you were able to simply stop the relentless march of activity for a moment and slip into the eternal space of *absolute rest*.

That's where you can drink from infinity and taste the source of all energy. Now, the paradox is that you can't "do" this, but you can practice relaxing into it.

Have fun.

DAY 18

deceleration time

One of the main reasons people in modern cultures can't sleep is the velocity they carry into their evening hours. Life has become fast, and we're all riding that wave all day. We're getting more done and are busier than ever, but when the craziness of that lifestyle washes up on the beach of our sleep, we get frustrated and unnerved. We don't leave time for deceleration. This means slowing down to *allow* for sleep.

Sleep is something that we release to. It happens on its own. We don't "do" sleep. Sleep happens when we relax into it and drop thoroughly into a slumber. The challenge of the modern world is that we race all day and into our evening. We watch our shows, make our calls, pay some bills, and then attempt to slam on the brakes and fall asleep when we finally get into bed. Nature doesn't work that way, and last time I checked, we come from nature.

Today's preliminary practice is to pay close attention to your evening rituals as they turn the corner toward sleep. What are you doing during the 3 to 4 hours prior to bedtime, and is it relaxing? The body and mind need some *deceleration* before sleep comes to us. Our ancestors had little access to additional light once the sun went down. That meant less stimulation and less activity leading up to bedtime. What are you doing to slow down in the evenings?

Blueshifted light on our screens, upbeat music, countless electronics, and mental stimulation are suffocating the quiet darkness of the night. Caffeine after 2 p.m. doesn't help either. We live in a world that is crowding out the peaceful energy of the nighttime hours. It is on you to bring this balance back into your life.

Look at your evenings and see what changes you can make to slow things down. Can you hang out by candlelight on most evenings? Maybe it's time to get into a good book instead of binge watching another TV series. Move toward stretching and real conversation instead of mindless entertainment and further stimulation.

Once you do this, you'll slowly start to see improved quality of sleep. Your days will begin with more energy and enthusiasm, and your stress levels will begin to come down. This is because your mind *needs* some slow time for processing and relaxation. Slamming on the brakes has a cost, and we're seeing it in our lives. That's not how sleep happens healthfully, and that's not how we best recover from our long, hard days. Build some yin mellowness into your evenings (especially weeknights) so your yang go time is more productive and better balanced.

Tonight's exercise is to do some mild stretching, about 30 minutes, prior to your desired bedtime. Bring down the lights and settle into your body. Brush your teeth and do all of your prebed rituals first, because after 5 to 10 minutes of stretching, you're to move to your bed. Lie flat on your back and start breathing down to your lower abdomen. After a few breaths, begin a progressive relaxation from your head down to your toes: Take your time and simply relax each body part, muscle, joint, organ, and region deeply as you scan down your body. When you've reached your toes, simply continue to take deep breaths down to your lower abdomen while slowly counting down from 10 to 1. Tell yourself that you are getting more relaxed and feeling heavier with each number you count down. When finished, simply allow yourself to drift into sleep.

This exercise is powerful but should be coupled with good sleep-hygiene rituals. It is up to you to slow down time and decelerate.

Understanding the different quality of time and how to roll with natural rhythms are the key lessons here.

DAY 19

cutting people who
suck your time

Today we deal with the time vampires in our life. You know who they are. They are the people who through conversation, drama, neediness, or some genuine problem, latch onto you and take you away from your plan for your day (or week or life). They are often people close to us, but we've entered a codependent relationship with them. The time together becomes wasted and doesn't serve us (or them) when we feel more tired, stressed, edgy, or even upset after hanging with them.

Your time is the measure of your life force, and it's all you have. Spending it recklessly with people who don't serve and support your mission in life is an easy way to feel empty, drained, and derailed. If you sense that the days are going by and you're not feeling better or getting closer to your goals, then it's time to investigate and find where the time is leaking.

Today make a list of the people you spend the most time with. From your family to people in your carpool to coworkers to random people you bump into, take an aggregate look at where your time goes in an average day. Do you spend a little too much energy hanging around the water cooler? Is the person in the cubicle across from you always talking to you about a show or event that doesn't mean much to you? Are there people who don't know the important things going on in your life, despite your knowing every intimate detail of theirs?

Ask yourself where you may be trying to be polite a little too often with your time. Do you entertain conversations or interactions that don't serve you? Do you know how to protect yourself from the people who drain you so that you're not spending your energy on them without getting anything in return? That's the first place to start.

Most time vampires have terrible energy hygiene and need to pass the time talking about stupid shit. They need someone like you to go tumbling down those rapids with them. Are you guilty of enabling this?

We all are to some extent. We've mistaken being nice with self-sacrifice.

This doesn't mean avoiding genuine conversations that fill you and enhance your day; it doesn't even mean cutting out all but the most critical interactions. It means holding the line and taking your time back. There are lots of great ways to do this, and most revolve around healthy boundaries. You need to find ways to excuse yourself from interactions that pull you away from your goals for today so you can stay focused. Get your work finished and then maybe go for a run with this person in a way that makes the interaction productive.

The challenge in front of you is that most people are stuck and need someone to be stuck with. That way, it's less lonely.

Avoid this at all costs.

You have dreams and aspirations. You never nap. You want to exercise. You have people whom you'd rather speak with. Find the places where you feel your time is being sucked and start pulling it back. It may feel awkward at first, but this practice will change your life.

It is your time. Stop leaking it away to nonsense.

DAY 20

big life events

L ife's quality of time isn't always the same. There are big things that come on occasion that hold a special place in our memories. Some events can be notable, but what about babies being born? Weddings and funerals are big. Graduations matter. What about winning big games or exiting marriages? These are all memorable days—not always good ones but certainly memorable.

Think back on your big life events. How present were you for them? What visual and auditory memories can you recall from those events, not only because you've seen the pictures but also because you can remember the experience? Could you grasp the magnitude of what was happening?

What big life events do you have coming? Are you excited for them? Are you ready?

Today spend some time looking back at the eventful and meaningful days of your past and then looking ahead to the future. How can you better prepare to be fully present and absorb the day as it unfolds? What can you learn about previous big days and how you handled them?

This exercise begets a bigger question. How can we stack more amazing and memorable days in our future? If looking down the timeline of your life shows nothing but boredom and monotony, what can you start to do to bring some excitement and life in?

We need a spark to look forward in life. Where is yours? Can you plan an adventure, get a degree, or take a trip with a spouse or a child? The trick is to not just look forward to a future date that may be memorable but to jump out and do something new and out of your comfort zone *today*. Then start making a plan for an even bigger adventure soon. Think it through and focus on what you'd like to see and feel on your special day. Connect with the feeling and visualize it. Once you've done so, it's time to start planning to make that idea manifest. Go after it.

What you've done is plant a seed in your timeline. It may take years to see the fruit, but now it is there. *Water it with your intent and goodwill.* Nourish this seed with action and movement in its direction. If you really want it, see it and feel it as if it is happening now. Hold that feeling in your heart. That's enough to plant the seed.

Over time, as you learn to connect with your inner self better, it'll get easier to go from seed to fruit in less time. For now know that the seed is in your future timeline. Keep it there. Send it love and nourish it. With this practice, you can increase the positive big life events in your timeline and give yourself a whole lot of goodness to reflect back on in your twilight years.

Think big and go for it!

DAY 21

family time

How often do we mix family time with other time? This way we're kind of hanging with our loved ones and kind of checking e-mail, watching a show, reading a book, and whatever else. It usually doesn't satisfy either well. Now, if you're in a situation where you can snuggle up with your loved ones and read together and enjoy the space, then great. You've got it good. The rest of the world struggles with the balance here.

Today let's lean into family time and make it special. Instead of trying to multitask while being with the family (especially kids), let's give them our all today.

What does this look like? Maybe a long walk with the dogs. It means dinner with no TV or devices. It could look like a play date, some intimate time, a hike, or a fireside hangout. Communicate with your family that you want to spend some quality time with them today, even if for a few minutes, then work to get it in.

Chances are, if you have older kids, everyone else is crazy busy, too, and they are just as time-deprived as you are. Welcome to the modern world. In this case, look for *quality of time* versus *quantity of time*. You may not have an hour to hang back, but connecting during a few minutes in the car (when nobody is looking at a screen) or catching up over dinner (when everyone's at the table at the same time) can go a long way. Once you set this as a precedent, you can work toward this goal more and more over the ensuing months. It may turn into a family vacation or something with more hang time.

Don't make it weird or sticky: Simply state that everybody's going to be trying something new for a few minutes from now on, and stick with it. Be present and share love. This sets an example and helps create the space for others to join. If it feels like your new agenda, it doesn't ring as authentic.

If you have kids, wait till they get to bed and hang with your partner (or the pets) once things have settled down. Get some unplugged time together and simply connect over what's going on with you. There's been precious little time for this in our lives, and our relationships have suffered. If you live alone, call a family member or loved one.

Today you're taking it back. You cherish your family and loved ones. Show them. Connect with them. This is time together you'll never get back. Savor it. Appreciate it.

DAY 22

time to digest

Your body likes to slow down around food. Your brain needs to register the smell, texture, flavor, and consistency of a meal to satisfy its needs. If it doesn't get a chance to do that, it'll keep sending signals to get more food, even if the stretch receptors of your gut are screaming over the huge lunch you've just pounded. That's how we've evolved and adapted.

Today your gong practice is to slow down around every meal.

The next step is to savor each morsel. Slow down and chew at least 10 times for every bite. *Taste* your food. Break it down. Our stomach acid, pancreatic enzymes, and gut bacteria are great at what they do, but they need our teeth and saliva to do their part first. If they don't, it puts undue stress on them and we eventually end up with digestive issues. These digestive issues lead to malabsorption and lower energy levels. Less energy means less time to get stuff done. Eating quickly actually drains our energy and robs us of time, according to that math.

On a spiritual level, today's the day to connect with the meal in front of you. Where did this food come from? Was it recently alive? Did it live well? Is it full of vitality, or did it come from some machine? This food will become the makeup of who you are in the next few days and weeks. It'll build every cell in your body and power your brain and immunity.

This means today is a day to give thanks to the life forms (plant or animal) that gave their lives so that you could continue yours. Yes, that's heavy, and we need to treat it accordingly.

Jamming through meals leads to a slow and painful spiritual death for us. Your task today is to stop time around each meal and appreciate the sacred act of eating. It'll help you digest, assimilate, and power your cells better. It'll also help you take a break from the crazy-train march of time that's been slobbering into your mealtime.

Take it back.

Mealtime is sacred, and we've forgotten this. It is valuable time and restorative in nature. You need this little pause in the insanity so you can navigate your day better. You need this discipline if you're going to master time. Your body needs time to do its job.

Slow down and enjoy your meals today.

DAY 23

podcasts and audiobooks

Now we're going to delve into finding some leverage in life. How? Through information. Today we take control of the information that you're exposed to by creating some simple but important filters in your world. We start with the information pollution we're exposed to every day. It makes no sense to sit there senselessly as you get bombarded with commercials and programming you don't care for.

There are a number of podcasting platforms out there to choose from. iTunes is the major one for most Apple devices, but there is Google Play, Stitcher, SoundCloud, and several other players for Android devices. You can listen on your phone while in your car or stream at your desk at work or in the kitchen. Most books can be found in audiobook format today.

Podcasts and audiobooks are great because you get to listen to them on *your time*. You can pick and choose the ones you want to consume and line them up for your commutes or workouts. You can play them at a fast speed and, basically, either learn something at twice the speed or decide to roll slower and hang out in a conversation that serves, entertains, or nourishes you.

Once you've found some content you can vibe with, look to see how it enriches your life. Learning from people gives us leverage, and this is an important concept. If someone is telling a part of their life story in a book or on a podcast, those are several years of experiences lived, learned, and summed up by another human who is imparting the wisdom gleaned from that time they spent. You are essentially getting all that life experience in a digestible package, which can go into your mind and help you make better decisions and simply navigate life better. From whom would you like to learn? What wisdom can you gather with your valuable time that will accelerate your growth, cut your stress, or help you steer clear of some bad decisions? That's leverage. A person's whole life experience summed up in an hour—that's good. Today you will take a step in that direction by curating the content you consume.

There are plenty of genres, including health, self-help, history, comedy, and much more. The key is to browse around and find content that enriches your life. It is all about *curation,* and you get to honor your time. Once you get into the habit of this, you'll feel more in control and be able to pick how you spend it.

There are lots of podcasts that talk about current events, contemporary issues, and social hot buttons. Books cover everything. What are you in the mood for? This is a time to step outside of your comfort zone and learn something new or to finally get a chance to catch up on that thing you've been meaning to check out but have never made the time. Maybe the answer is silence—that's cool, but today's exercise is to spend a few minutes browsing around and finding at least one podcast you can listen to next time you *have the time* to listen to something.

Sitting in a position of power allows you to choose what information goes into your head. Learning to master time is a process, and a big part of this process is controlling the flood gates. Don't let outside influences waste your time ever again. Pick the content you choose to consume. If it gets stale or boring, then move on to something else. The key is that *you are driving.* Act like it.

DAY 24

communication

Much of the time we spend on our devices nowadays can be considered communication. From calls to texts to e-mails to social media, we're technically communicating with other people in some way. Even if we're putting a statement out to the world, that's a form of communication.

Today let's kick it a bit old school. Let's roll back to how our species used to communicate before technology. Of course there was the spoken word, but we've also interacted with a variety of nonverbal ways for millennia.

Your gong today is to become aware of these. From hand gestures to eye movements, notice all the ways people in your world get their point across. A sigh, a shoulder shrug, an intentional stare, and a timely cough are all ways we say things as well.

Watch for this today. People who are hearing impaired are amazing at this. They watch and actually *see* so much that we've become numb to. People who are visually impaired are amazing at detecting the nuances of sound. They hear things we're oblivious to. Why? Because they are far more attuned to these senses.

Today's gong is to flex some of this capacity yourself. Observe others. Try to use nonverbal means of communication with people and see how that works. If you need to speak, choose brevity and elegance in your words. Say more with less. Make it a game.

We've become too numb. Your task today is to wake back up and pay more attention to your surroundings. With so much talk about mindfulness out there, most people think this work needs to happen on a meditation cushion exclusively. Life is the workshop of mindfulness. Pay attention and take it in today. Watch how people around you are communicating, and try to interface with them in varied ways. See how things shift.

Play with it and enjoy.

DAY 25

dealing with to-do lists

It's hard to get lots of things done without a to-do list nowadays. The list is something you make to keep yourself on track. These are items that you have said need to get done in order for you to progress in your life. There is nothing intrinsically wrong with these lists. In fact, they're great. So why do they cause so much stress for people?

The answer is simple. Most people don't complete their items, so the list leaves them feeling like they have, on some level, failed.

The question for today's lesson is whether you're overcommitting to too many items on a list or whether you're not executing efficiently to get through the list. In my experience, it's usually a combination of the two. That means that you've probably gotten in the habits of both biting off more than you can (or should) chew and also not staying focused on checking off items and moving through your work. Take 5 minutes to sit with your to-do list(s) and determine whether you find it to be realistic. Are you dragging items from last week (or month) forward into today? Why are you not getting to them? Do you actually need to be handling this stuff? If not, then delegate. If yes, then what's the issue that's preventing you from addressing them?

Big items that don't get finished have a tremendous weight to them. They burden our minds. If you're dragging these forward, then maybe it's time to commit to less on your current workload to get caught up. What corners can you cut to dig through the mess that you're in? What can you let go of, and what must remain? Once you've determined what must remain, it's time to make a plan and stick to it. Maybe you need to burn the midnight oil for a little while until you've powered through the project that's been causing you to fret. The burden of yesterday's worries that are with us today is heavy. It is time to make a plan to reconcile and find peace. Committing to powering through to the end is not the worst plan when you consider how much mental, emotional, and spiritual strain you've been under by carrying the past forward—as long as you treat that strategy as a temporary event rather than a lifestyle.

If you have challenges with motivation, that's usually a function of focus, attention, and energy. Getting yourself into a daily fitness routine can break the monotony. Get moving and shake things up a bit. The biggest issue is carrying time debt forward and not seeing a way out.

Making a plan is only half the battle. *Sticking to the plan is the hard part.* Sure, accidents happen and there's an occasional setback, but pushing things to Friday is unhealthy. Today's goal is to make a plan for your to-do list and then follow it to the letter.

The best way to get things done is piecemeal. Go through your calendar today and set goals for each half day (as a chunk of time) and work to get them finished. Be realistic with your expectations of yourself, and couple this with a healthy work ethic that's sustainable. Be finished by the end of each day so you can go home and feel like you're ready to enjoy some personal or family time. If you're way behind, make a *time-debt repayment plan* and suck it up until you're caught up. Like money, you have to see where the time is bleeding and shore up any loose ends. This practice will make you better at committing to new items on your timeline. It'll help you get real and stay real with yourself.

We all have lots of work to do. That's fine. How we deal with it determines whether we thrive or are crushed under the weight of our burdens. Today you need to make the right choice and take control of your time.

DAY 26

when to go all out

Not all time is created equal. There are times of the day, times of the week, seasons of the year, and even eras in your life when you need to lean into things and devote more hours to your career or projects. That's natural.

In the old days, we'd hunt at twilight or dawn, when the animals were going for a drink. At midday, we'd rest out of the hot sun. When we started farming, we'd plant, till the soil, and harvest at appropriate times. We'd usually have the winters to rest, recover, and catch our breath. Things were tied to nature, and we moved with these cycles. At harvesttime, it was all hands on deck, with lots of long, hard hours.

What about now? Artificial lights, temperature control, frozen food, and insane deadlines keep us spinning without any built-in recovery time. We get no rest cycles, and we push too hard. The old saying "Make hay while the sun shines" is appropriate in our lives today, when we ought to be paying closer attention than ever to the natural rhythms of our energy and attention.

So how do we carefully plan our exertion for the maximum results and more playtime?

That's today's lesson. Most people have the best energy in the mornings. That usually couples with clarity, enthusiasm, and drive. If that's you, then plan your day to get the most critical tasks finished in the early part of the day. If you're the type who needs a few hours to boot up, then maybe midday or early afternoon is best for you.

Although not advisable for most, some people simply turn on in the evenings and that's when they get their best work done. If that's you, then how have you arranged your life to factor that in?

The key is to know when you're at your best and plan your important business or tasks to happen then. Look at your lifestyle today and see how your day is stacked. Is there something planned for 4 p.m. that makes you cringe? How about the work you're planning on doing tonight after the kids go down? Some of it is unavoidable in the short term, but let's take a hard look at these patterns today and see what can be changed.

Go through your calendar (and maybe this has to be a month out) and start moving things around when you can. Many successful people block off time from 8 a.m. to 11 a.m. for their most important work. You can build in small breaks every 30 to 60 minutes, but hold your calls, avoid e-mail, mute the phone for texts, get into whatever you set aside for that time block, and *get it done.*

Here's the thing about getting things done: It gives us peace of mind. Why? Because that to-do item is now cleared out of your mind and finally handled. It no longer plagues you and sits in the back of your mind. Think about this concept today.

How much of your stress comes from overwork, and how much can be attributed to inefficiencies you can work on? How would you feel if you were better at closing out tasks and feeling accomplished on a daily basis? Could you then go home and relax more easily? Perhaps you'd be more present with your family?

Absolutely.

Take a look at where you can schedule your make-hay time today, and look into the future on your calendar. Make the adjustments when you can, and take notice of what happens. When we were young, we'd get to go out and play when our homework was finished. How long has it been since you've had that experience? Work hard when you have the energy, and then relax and play hard without the guilt.

DAY 27

eternal time

The ancient religions and philosophies of the world talk about eternity a whole lot. It's easy for us to hear this and think, "Oh, sure, heaven and that afterlife, nirvana stuff, yeah, yeah," and move on with our day. Today let's slow down and take a look at what eternity implies.

The mere fact that we're trying to speak of the term is a challenge. As we define something, we help make it definite so that we can isolate what it is versus what it isn't and wrap our brains around it. Making something known requires us to draw a circle around it so our minds can grasp it conceptually.

So how do we do that with the concept of *infinity*?

Eternity implies infinity. It is portrayed by a horizontal number eight, and the line folds back on itself in perpetuity. It's hard to define something that doesn't slow down or stop for us. You can't grasp the wind.

When the ancients spoke of eternal time, we have to assume *they meant it*. They spoke of a place in which time and space don't exist. Whether you call it heaven or transcendence, this place is timeless and filled with potential. This puts us in a semantic quagmire where we speak of places like heaven where there's eternal time. But do we truly grasp what we're implying? Eternity means no end.

Let's spend some time with this concept today. If you were to roll with the assumption that your spirit or consciousness is eternal, what would that say about you? That means there's *never an end to you*. The person you truly are has always been here and will always remain. Outside time, there *you* are. Your existence has no beginning and no end, so it lives in an endless stream of time that is nonlinear.

Think about this. Think long and hard.

We're so set on defining things in terms of the present and understanding reality that eternity breaks our minds. We can't think about it, because, frankly, there's nothing there. That doesn't mean that *everything* isn't embedded in the *nothing,* and vice versa.

Spend some time contemplating the essence of infinity today. What does it mean to be truly eternal? What part of you would pass on and through? If you were to imagine who you'd be 5,000 years from now, what would that look like? If you could never die, how would that change the way you see today?

How can you recollect and connect with your eternal self? Your body will pass. It'll push up flowers and be long gone, but what about the spirit inside, the consciousness that dwells in your heart? Where does that go? Where is it right now? How can you connect with it?

That is the real work.

Dig deep and connect with the "I" behind the artificial constructs and ego defenses. Dig deep into who you really are.

Your life's work should revolve around finding this, cultivating its presence, and solidifying your connection with it. Your eternal self is the gem you've been looking for, and it is inside you. When you whittle away all the noise and pretending, you will find the real you. Take the time to reflect on this today and your relationship with time will never be the same.

The eternal aspect of you is the real you.

DAY 28

time to catch your breath

Today let's recall that feeling you get when you've been doing cardio and you have to stop to catch your breath. This is something that doesn't sneak up on you if you're aware of your body, but we've all been there—on the side of the court (or trail), panting and waiting to recover.

Long-distance runners, swimmers, soccer players, and pretty much all elite athletes know that the key to avoiding getting stuck in this position is to *stay under your breath*. This means not getting so far ahead of yourself that you need to stop for recovery. That requires awareness of the line. We all have one, and it tends to move depending on the number of hours we've slept, food we've eaten, stress we're under, age we are, and whether we are sick.

Now let's think about this in the context of your life. Do you live your life like it is a series of sprints where you then have to pull over and pant? Is that the best way to roll?

Most of us live on the edge and often cross the line daily, stumbling home to collapse on the sofa after spending it all at work. Or maybe we're already panting by the time we even get to work, and that's why it feels like balls are always dropping at the office. Maybe we're running so hard from the personal problems we're facing that we don't have anything left to give to our loved ones.

Today your task is to ask yourself honestly how you've been running your life. What's your line today? How much energy can you reasonably exert and still feel like you've got gas in the tank, can stay in a good mood, and have enough resilience to fend off a minicrisis or whatever else life throws at you? What is it going to take to stay under your breath and be able to handle your daily work without faltering? Do you need to slow down a bit? Maybe take on fewer items and do the things in front of you with better clarity and focus? What do you need to adjust in order to be able to do that?

When running a 200-mile distance, sprinting out the gate and blowing out your energy doesn't get you to the destination. Life is long. You have to be there for your family. You have many more years you should enjoy on this planet. Are you running at a pace that's in conflict with that? Take a cold, hard look.

Start making a list of the things you need to throttle down on, and then map out some ideas on how you think you can do that. It may take some conversations with people at work or maybe your family. Making adjustments is a mark of maturity. Runners learn to pace themselves. Sprinters are super relaxed before their race. Look at what it takes to strike this balance in your life, because when you *are* staying under your breath, something magical happens. The quality of time slows down, and things feel Zen-like. The compressed time that comes with sprint-and-pant lifestyles feels more stressed. It is more stressed. Find a rhythm that will work long term and remember to stay under your breath. It'll change your life.

DAY 29

deathbed wisdom

We seldom hear from people who are dying that they regret not working enough. It's usually regrets about time lost working and away from loved ones. Maybe they regret alienating people close to them or losing themselves somewhere along the way. It is always something deeper and more human.

What about you? Have you ever stopped to check your bearings? Well—that's today's practice.

Take a few minutes today and sit down in a quiet place. Close your eyes and start breathing to your lower abdomen. Take a minute to settle in and relax.

Now from here, start to think about yourself in the future, lying on your deathbed, thinking back about the years you've lived. What are you grateful for? What brought you the most joy? Think about this and feel the feelings. Sit with them.

Now go the other way. What regrets do you have? Where do you feel like you wasted your time and your life force? Was it worth it? How did you go down that road, and what could have been avoided? Where did you get stuck and pulled off your life's path? Is it painful? Feel it. Sit with it.

Spend some time here and get clear about what you're witnessing. Allow the emotions to sweep over you. Let them sink in.

Now it's time to rewire something. Pick up a pen and pad (or take notes in this book or on your phone).

If your *future self* were speaking to your current self from her deathbed, what advice would she be giving you?

- What would she have you steer clear of?
- What would she ask that you lean into?
- Where should you spend your energy?
- Where does she think you're wasting your time and life?

Allow this dialogue to come through. Feel it. Listen.

What does your future self think about where you are now and how you're spending your precious time? Could you be doing things differently? Maybe making some better decisions? Maybe it'll take awhile to get out of the mess that you're in, but what are the next few steps you need to take to move into a better direction?

Promise your future self that you won't waste your life. Promise that you'll shift and change the way you roll so you can eradicate those painful regrets. *Commit* to making those changes and decide what your next logical step would be. *Take that step today.*

From time to time, close your eyes and go back to this scene. Are you on track? Looking back from your deathbed, are you making changes and moving in the right direction? Can you see a smile on your future self's face as that reality becomes manifest? Good. If not, then make adjustments!

This practice can be your guiding light for years to come. It'll help you stay on track and invest your time in the right people, activities, dreams, and possibilities.

DAY 30

gardening

One of the best ways to slow down and connect with the earth is gardening. It teaches us patience and helps us understand the cycles of life. It takes a while for a seed to sprout and depending on the type of plant, up to a few months to see the intended results. Some fruit trees take years to mature before there's a payout.

Good things come to those who wait, despite the vibe of our culture to go as fast and far as we can until we drop. We're driven to want instant satisfaction in today's world, and nothing is fast enough. We grow impatient when a Web page takes an extra second to load and honk if someone in front of us lags in taking off from a red light.

Gardening helps temper this tendency.

We grow to understand that life takes time to grow and natural rhythms are cyclical. There's a time to plant and a time to harvest. There's a time to work all day and a time to rest.

Today get into your garden. If you have one already, spend real, uninterrupted time tending it: Examine the leaves, smell the soil, prune and cut if necessary, and observe how each living thing is growing. If you don't have access to any living thing, it's time to go shopping. It could be a single tomato plant or a countertop cactus in a bowl if you lack space. The point is to connect with a plant or a seed (which carries life energy and information) and nurture it.

Growth is slow but steady.

The right conditions are necessary for success.

Gardening brings sanity to our life and gives us a powerful natural metaphor to run as a filter against the *insanity* of modern life. There is a ritual in keeping a plant alive—having to water it, check its soil, and give it the same kind of care on a regular basis. Slow down and enjoy the process. Set goals for a season and plan on making sure it'll be an abundant harvest. Look ahead and *plan ahead* so you can offset the stress that comes from unreasonable expectations of yourself. Get your hands in the dirt, and touch the life that lives in the soil.

Connect with life.

There's a powerful circuit that gets activated when we touch the dirt and connect with life in an elemental fashion. You'll know it when you've experienced it. If you already have, then get back in the dirt. If this is all new to you, well, enjoy the amazing experience you're about to have.

DAY 31

framework before work

There's an old saying among carpenters: "Measure thrice, cut once." This may seem like more work up front but helps avoid costly mistakes that suck both time and money. It is a measured approach to life that includes a word that's all but lost in our lexicon: planning.

It's so easy to make hasty decisions nowadays. Marketing drives us to be impulsive and buy things before we consider their overall worth or value to us. This has now spilled over into multiple areas of our lives where we go for it and jump into the water before checking the depth.

Today let's slow down a bit. In business, there's another saying that insists on "framework before work." This implies that if we map out our trajectory and make a plan, then the work becomes self-evident and far easier. At the other end of it, failing to plan is planning to fail.

Let's look at your life today in this context.

Are you doing things that are reactive to your immediate circumstances? How much time do you spend circling back to undo your snap decisions? For instance, how often do you find yourself needing to go to the mall to return things you decided you don't need? That's valuable time today fixing yesterday's bad decisions. What about with injuries? Did you hit the court without stretching again? The joint pain and stiffness then creep up and make it hard to keep exercising.

Perhaps you took 2 hours this week to get a massage and have been icing daily since the incident. Was that worth it versus taking 10 minutes to stretch in the first place?

Look for examples like this in your life. It's easy to be penny-wise and dollar-foolish with our time. It usually comes back to bite us.

In the context of work, how much time do you spend planning your next move or organizing your priorities rather than launching ahead toward the e-mail at the top of your inbox? If you have tons of work in front of you, do you start shoveling and have at it, or can you make a plan of attack? This is where some time spent doing top-down thinking can go a long way. Whiteboards are great for this. However you need to organize your thoughts, the key is to create some structure to then fill it in with your energy. Leave time for planning, mind mapping, and strategizing in your week. Get into your calendar and block off some chunks of time for this today.

What would life be like if you didn't have to go back and clean up multiple messes each week? How much more would you accomplish in a day if you only ever had to work on or think about a task once rather than executing, tweaking, and revising several times before you moved on?

Remember, spending energy is like spending time or money. It can simply fly out of you. The wisdom comes in learning to direct your time, money, and energy in ways that serve you.

DAY 32

listening to noise

We live in a world that bombards us with sound. It's everywhere, and we've grown accustomed to noise pollution in our daily lives. Back in the day, we'd listen to the sounds of the animals. This was a vast communication channel that informed us of the location of both predators and our next meal. Today, aside from a screeching car tire or ambulance sound, there isn't much useful information in all the noise around us. It does, however, still impact us. Our brains register it, and somewhere deep inside, we have to process the "is this safe?" flag it raises. This is exhausting after some time. Why? Because sound is frequency based. It flows in waves and at different velocities, and these hit us and impact us whether we consciously feel them or not. After all, we're over 60 percent water: Imagine how those waves would ripple through every cell of your body.

Time is also frequency based; it is rhythmic. How do you think the constant bombardment of your senses by these sound waves would affect your perception of time? Would it agitate it? Would it speed it up? Slow it down? It all depends on the symphony of sound you're in and your recognition of it. It's like time soup. Next time you're in a public area today, simply stop and listen to the ambient noise all around you. Is it comforting, or is your body somehow telling you, "Get me out of here." Kids can't filter the noise, and you'll notice how a small child will get agitated in a crazy-hectic place. The noise is unsettling.

We adults? Well, we've developed layers of psychological defenses—we cope and stay put—but why? How is the noise agitating your mind and shifting your ability to relax into time?

Stop to feel this today. Take a few seconds to take in the sounds all around you. Do this several times today and just *feel* what's going on inside you.

If you determine that some noise is disruptive, you can leave, ask people to shut up, get noise-canceling headphones, or play your own music to superimpose a frequency pattern and override it. The moral of the story is to not stand there and take it on the chin. Nobody is strong enough to go unscathed in noise pollution. It's just a matter of when and how you crack.

What's the point of punishing yourself? To own your experience and have mastery over time, today listen to the noise wherever you go and ask yourself:

"Does this make me feel good or bad?"

"Is it unsettling or nourishing?"

"Can I relax deeply in here, or are there arrows flying at me?"

You may not be able to run out of there, but this practice will help you become far more aware of the space that you're in and the *quality* of time in that space. Once you have your bearings in space and time, well, you know where you stand and can make the right move. You'll also develop an acute awareness of how noise affects your mood.

Stop and listen.

DAY 33

time on the ground

W hen's the last time you hung out on the ground? That's where our ancestors spent most of their downtime. Whether it was sitting around a fire, beading in a circle, crouching on a hunt, or sleeping on a mat, our forefathers were constantly in intimate contact with the ground.

This does wonderful things for the body and mind. For the body, it helps us use postural muscles to hold ourselves up (without the props of modern furniture). It helps us open our lower limbs and hips and gives us feedback about where our bodies may be tight.

For the mind, it helps connect us with an endless flow of negatively charged ions that come from the earth. This not only helps offset inflammation in our bodies but also connects us with a powerful current of energy—that of the earth.

The Schumann resonances are the frequency of background noise all around us. They come from the natural environment and tend to hover at about 7.83 hertz. This is similar to the alpha rhythm of the brain. The alpha wave range (8 to 12 hertz) is often associated with meditation and relaxed states of consciousness. In brain labs, seasoned meditators who are being mapped by EEG electrodes tend to be strong in this frequency range during practice.

Fancy that. The earth is already vibrating at an ideal wavelength. Some time on the ground allows us to sync up with this and slow down to a more sane time stamp that can be akin to meditation. The velocity of modern living often has us revving in high gear, and the people around us are also caught in it, so crazy is the new normal.

Not for you. Not today.

Get on the floor and spend about 15 minutes there. Take off your shoes and sit on the ground. Ideally you allocate this time to some stretching, rolling around, sitting cross-legged, or however else you want to hang out. Get comfy on the floor and slow down. Feel the earth under you, and slow down your breath to sync up with it. Don't check your phone or get wrapped up watching TV. Hang out and see how you feel. At first, it'll seem awkward and boring. That's the crazy talking. You are better when relaxed. You are better when in sync with the natural environment.

Avoid any screen time while doing this practice. The technosphere is insane; don't live there. Just visit when you need to. Live with nature. Feel it under your body, and allow yourself to slow down during this practice. Technology is a tool; don't mistake the tool for reality.

Slow isn't weak. That's a toxic meme. You can draw power from the earth, and that can keep you going at a healthier clip for the rest of the day.

Today you practice a homecoming with planet Earth.

Sit down and unwind for a few.

DAY 34

smiling

Today's gong is simple: You're going to practice smiling all day long. It doesn't need to be weird or over the top, but get into a mindset that commits you to bridging the gap between yourself and others with a simple smile.

Why? Because we're hardwired to respond favorably to smiles. It is an icebreaker and a mood softener. Look around you. Most people are stumbling through their days with worried minds and furrowed brows. You've probably been one of them recently.

Today we break this.

Every time you establish eye contact with another person, gift them with a warm smile from the bottom of your heart. Do it unconditionally. This means you can't get pissed if they don't respond, frown, or don't reciprocate. That's their problem. Your job is to simply spread warmth and love one smile at a time as you roll through your day.

If you're the type who doesn't get much human contact in an average day, make a point of going somewhere people tend to gather, and practice this gong today. Walk around and do your thing with a smile on your face.

See what is different by day's end. How do you feel? Is your mood any different than it would be on a normal day? How so?

Did you make any friends or strike up conversations that were nourishing? Become mindful of the reactions you got.

A smile can melt a glacier at the right time and place. You can change someone's stars with this practice. You may have saved a suicide or shifted someone's day toward a better decision. Tiny acts of beauty can carry far beyond our ability to track or understand them.

Let the warmth fly and see how your day shakes out.

DAY 35

drinking from infinity

Where does energy come from? Why do we feel better when we take a break and rest for a few minutes? Where are we restoring ourselves from?

Today is the day you get to stop and think about this. In the stillness of the present moment, you have an opportunity to access amazing time and space that are always available to you. It's the place where you're not dwelling on your past or worrying about your future but are simply present, here and now. It's the state our spiritual masters talk about, and we maybe give it an intellectual nod and go back to our crazy days. Not today.

Today your gong item is to *stop time* and drink from infinity.

What does this mean?

It means checking in with yourself once every hour (set a timer on your phone or computer) and asking yourself this important question: "What am I doing right now?" Whatever the answer is, simply stop doing it, take a few breaths, and commit to deeply relaxing and doing nothing for 30 seconds. The exercise is more about learning where the dial is and simply playing with it (at first). Over time, you'll get better at this and feel what this state of "not doing" or "simply being" is. Right now it sounds crazy. That's fine. Take 30 seconds once per hour to stop and commit to relaxing deeply. It'll give you a glimpse.

A glimpse of what?

Of the infinite amount of energy, time, and potential that is locked in the stillness of the present moment. The mystics learned to mine for energy, clarity, wisdom, and blessings from this space, and we are hardwired with the same capacity to do so. We've simply forgotten.

Consider today your homecoming to a primordial state where you could draw upon vast reserves of energy deep within you. This space is only a conscious shift away. Once you find your way in, it'll be the greatest treasure you've ever known.

Now stop and drink . . . drink from infinity.

DAY 36

cutting existing commitments

L et's look at the ball of yarn we have in front of us today: our existing commitments. These start to accumulate over time, and we seldom do an audit of them to determine whether they still serve us. Some of these commitments are lifelong, some long-term, and others come and go. Unfortunately, some overstay their welcome and need to be swept out (but seldom are). Your marriage, your kids, your career, your health, and your relationships are all commitments. Today let's take a look at the ones that are serving us and the ones that tend to aggravate and drain us.

Make a list of the commitments you have in life. Jam down a page and write down all that come to mind. Dogs need to be fed, loved, and walked. A house has to be kept up. Older parents have lots of needs. Write down all the commitments you currently have. Once you get all the big stuff down, you will undoubtedly come up with more: the class you committed to taking, the book club you said you'd join, the renovation project that's under way. Anything you commit to is now on the list.

We make millions of little microcommitments every year. From saying yes to a ski trip to RSVPing to a wedding to opting into an online summit to simply buying a book—these are all commitments. You certainly didn't buy that book to place it on your nightstand and look at it, did you? If it takes you a month to get through a book, how many months of backlogged reading are you looking at? That's stressful on a subtle level: It's always there.

You see, these things add up pretty quickly once you start to list and stack up everything you've said yes to. Every little yes requires some of your attention, brainpower, soul, and time. Is it any wonder why most people are so tired?

How the hell are you going to get to all of this? That's the crisis of the modern world.

Too many commitments in too little time. If you want to master life, you need to be clear about your existing outlay of time and energy so you can know what's on your plate and use that as a *filter* to help you determine what else you can take on.

Today look at your tangled web of commitments and think about what isn't serving you. Can you back out? How can you do so gracefully? Maybe you need a phased exit from some, and that's fine. Look at where your time and mental energy is trapped, and then come up with a responsible exit plan for yourself. When you start doing this, you'll notice how challenging it is to change a yes to a no in many circumstances. This'll help you better say no to opportunities that don't serve you when they come up.

Think about how it would feel to clean out your time closet today. See how many hours per week you can liberate with this exercise, and make it a habit to practice good commitment hygiene. There's no vitality in a stressed-out life. There's no life to be lived if there's no time to enjoy.

DAY 37

workplace shuffle

Work is a place where we tend to drift into a dreary sleep. We show up and get busy with the tasks at hand. Our time gets sucked into our projects, and we hardly look up and remember to care for ourselves some days.

Today we stir the pot a bit. Move your pictures around on your desk. Look to rearrange the stuff on the walls. Move your whole workstation a bit if you can. The point is to hack your workplace environmentally to interrupt your pattern.

You are too familiar with your setting at your desk; this lulls us to sleep and dulls our senses. It actually robs us of spark and creativity. Spatial awareness cues our bodies to stay more awake and our brains to work in a more integrated fashion. This is good.

Move around what you can and make it so your space is now different. See how it feels. You may need to water some plants, light some sage, dust some pictures, or file away some stacks. That's healthy. Clutter numbs the mind. Blocked energy in your environment blocks the energy flowing through your life. You don't want that.

Mix it up today and see how you feel. From there, spend a few minutes thinking about what's in your way at work. Can you see through some places you've been stuck? Maybe it's time to clear your old to-do lists so you can also declutter your mental space?

What we see around us is often a mirror of our internal state. Fixing it from the outside in can be quite helpful.

Have fun with this.

DAY 38

daydreaming

Do you often catch yourself daydreaming? Where do you tend to go? What are you thinking about?

Oftentimes, we're replaying scenarios the way we would have liked them to occur or imagining ourselves doing something we're afraid of doing. Maybe you are off on some vacation, enjoying the sunshine away from the dreary life you're sitting in. Where do you go?

It is normal and healthy to daydream. It is a nice part of our human experience, but for many people, it has become disruptive and has taken over. We need creative outlets for our thoughts and emotions. We process much of this in our dreams at night, and unfortunately, lots of people have trouble sleeping. That means no night dreams, which then creates a need to spill over into the day. The brain needs the release.

For others, there's never been enough room to goof off or be creative. Our school system has been a big culprit in this. Show up, sit down, shut up, listen up, stay awake, take this test, and move to the next class: It leaves no room for imagination and creativity in a child's mind. We are those children.

Think about the last time you were daydreaming. Was it nice, or did it go too far? Were you processing old memories and digesting information, or were you simply flowing in the realm of imagination? Time debt has us constantly catching up on yesterday's thoughts. This is *mental indigestion,* and most of us are guilty of it because we stack events so tightly that we leave no time to process what just happened.

Well, it has to process sometime, and maybe that's where you went.

If daydreaming has gotten disruptive in your life, then you need to look at what you're not getting in your typical days and how you can maybe add some creative time to get it. Maybe you need to take more walks. Maybe you need to pick up that old paintbrush and honor your creativity. It is different for every person. What do you need?

There's nothing intrinsically wrong with daydreaming. Our ancestors used to take midday naps and simply hang around during the hottest hours. They'd be locked in huts during cold winters with no TV. Imagination, story, creativity, and, yes, daydreaming were a big part of how we spent our time. Where are you getting these outlets today? How can you build them in so you feel whole?

True, there are better times and places to daydream than others, and it may have become disruptive in your life. Where can you make room for this vital human need so you can stay focused at work? How can you shift your life around a bit to allow for a creativity pressure-release valve?

Today's exercise involves blocking off some time to play with day-dreaming. Think about a trip you'd like to take. Think about the sights, the sounds, the textures. Close your eyes and imagine being there. Now walk around and explore this realm in your mind. Smile and see this scenario play out. Take about 20 minutes to do this.

How do you feel afterward? It helps reduce stress and high beta wave activity in the brain. It allows the theta band frequency to boost up, and this helps create overall brain health in most busy people. Theta is a comfortable wavelength for the brain to hang out in from time to time. Think of it as a lower gear in a car that allows us to cruise and not crank the engine all the time.

Building daydreaming into your life can be incredibly therapeutic. Enjoy the process—oh, and, yes, you have permission to do so. Most people feel guilty about it. Don't.

DAY 39

time audit

Today we do an audit of where our time goes. Like being in debt, the first step to cleaning up a problem is to know where the losses are. Let's not leave any stone unturned. Jot down what you're doing throughout the day, and don't judge. Let's take a cold hard look at where your time is going.

The first step is to look at your calendar. Is it an accurate reflection of how your day rolls out? If not, how can you line it up with reality? Where are there blocks that flow off into random uses of your time?

From there, either in your phone or on a notepad, set a timer to go off every 15 minutes. Once you hear it, STOP and quickly jot down what you did in the *past 15 minutes*: Get as detailed as you need to, and jot down or star where you think you may be inefficient. Repeat this process for the entire day, from waking to bedtime.

This may seem like a pain, but you'll end up finding some valuable data in here. This isn't to say you're not allowed to relax or goof off. Not at all! In fact, the hope is to find more time to goof off *without any guilt*. How do we do this?

We take our time audit seriously.

Today look for places where we seem busy but don't net results. What can you do to get more efficient at work or chores so you could have more dedicated relaxed time in the day? Or maybe you never have time to exercise: This practice could help you retrieve those elusive 30 minutes that can change your life.

None of this means you have to become a robot and march through your day. It is simply an exercise in *awareness*. You need to know where your valuable life energy (measured in time) is going in order to determine whether you are happy with it or not. If so, then great—you're in good shape. If not, however, this practice will turn up a handful of places you could start working on in life.

Get better at being aware and present.

DAY 40

time and money

Trading time for money is something most people on the planet are stuck with. It sucks. It puts a dollar amount on your time, which is actually a metric of your life. When your time is up, your life is over. Putting a value on that is challenging and, frankly, somewhat offensive.

Here's some quick math: If you earn $30 per hour and have 20 more years where you could work, you are getting paid just over $1.2 million for *the rest of your life*. Okay, you'll get a few hours with family, some sleep, and your weekends, but the point is, that's your value to society or the economy. Yes, that rate can go up with better-quality work, but today let's think about ways to liberate you from the time-for-money trade.

Can you do a project online that can earn more money on the side? Sure, it may take several hours to set up and oversee, but how can you automate and scale it to make money while you sleep? Can you invest in some real estate to cash out and reinvest so your capital can work for you? If so, look into it.

The point is to realize that time for money is limiting and, especially with the Internet, there are options. When you can do this, the extra money you make can *buy back* some of the time you need to work. You can then go back to school, take a vacation, work out, or hang with your loved ones. The point is, you get that time back for *living life*.

Ideally, you create a gig where your passive revenue matches and then exceeds your bills. Once you're there, you can elect to work or not in your usual gig. You can use that income to bank money and buy a better future for yourself, or you can choose to chill out and garden all day. You are free.

That's the real promise of capitalism that has been lost in translation. You don't need more things to fill up your house. But what about time? If you could liberate your time and untie it from the clock at work, how would you spend it?

Think about this today. When you find some clarity, write it down and map it out. This clarity can give you a vision to work toward, and then you can sit down and reverse engineer what kind of income you'd need to offset your current job. If your vision is exciting enough, you'll use your enthusiasm to research options and find a way. It'll probably take lots of hard work to hatch this new vehicle (beware of get-rich-quick bullshit), but eventually, you'll see that the results and your time invested can result in *time freedom*.

Envision a life where you didn't need to trade time for money. Now walk into that vision and make a plan.

DAY 41

prayer

P rayer used to be a central part of life. Most people did it daily and found much peace, connection, and solace in the ritual. Today droves of people have left mainstream religion and are looking for answers in a variety of places. There's a growing number of people inquiring and searching for truth and meaning, and this has led to many good things. Prayer, however, may be a baby-bathwater loss in this mix.

Multiple studies show the health benefits of prayer. It brings down our stress and helps ease our minds. If you are religious, it connects you with divinity and puts you in a wonderful place. If you're not, then this is a hard place to go. Perhaps today, then, becomes a day to practice gratitude.

The essence of prayer is often an opportunity to take some time and connect with God (or your higher self). There are so many traditions and opinions here, so without getting into the weeds, let's stay high level and do something that can help all of us here. If you have a tradition you're aligned with, do that.

Let's take 10 minutes and go to a quiet place. Make sure you can be left alone, which also means you should shut off your phone.

Put your hands together in front of your heart and put a smile on your face. Begin to breathe in and out of your heart, opening up this region and warming it up. Spend a couple minutes there.

Once you're nicely settled in, start to think about all the things you're grateful for in your life. Give thanks for them. Count your blessings.

Take a few minutes to do this, and then shift your attention to the life around you. Think of the people in your life whom you care for. Bring warmth to your heart as you think of them, and in your mind's eye, send love from your heart directly to theirs. Bathe them in love and appreciation. Hang here and scan your mind for people to love up today.

Now shift your attention to someone who may not be in your inner love circle but is in your life. Whomever this may be, let the first candidate pop up on your mental screen. You may not know why, but it doesn't matter. Bathe this person with love and kindness as well. Shower her with light and put a warm smile on your face.

If you have a practice based in some faith, move to whatever that practice is from here. If you don't, keep scanning for people in your world you can love up, and share the light with them.

Move back to giving thanks for what you have, the people in your life, and the opportunities you've been given.

Once you're ready to finish this, commit to devoting one random act of kindness today. Here's the key though: Make it anonymous. Do something nice and meaningful for someone in your world, but don't try to take credit for it. Make this your way of conducting charity and it'll free your ego from attachment.

Religious affiliations may be shifting, but our hearts should remain centered on goodness. Today find this, anchor in, and bring out the best in yourself *for others*.

DAY 42

people have different time stamps

H ave you ever encountered someone and suddenly felt *different?* Do some people calm you down and make you feel at ease while others agitate you or get under your skin?

Sometimes this has to do with the time stamp people are in. It's the vibratory frequency they are emitting. How fast are they vibrating? How loud are they being? Think of the sound of a fly buzzing by your ear. Too fast, agitating, and unnerving.

What about that clerk who can't seem to get that you've got places to be other than in the molasses of their presence? Yeah, that's a slower time stamp. If this is frustrating you today, think about how you can change or influence the situation in a better way.

The fact is, we all run at different speeds throughout the day, and some people, well, they've got a certain gear they like to run in. This may or may not serve us. Think of the coworker who crashes your relaxed vibe with his caffeine overdose. Slow it down, buddy.

So how do we adjust for this time differential? Step number one is to recognize it. *Feel* the quality of time in your own body and that of the person or people you're engaging with. Do you need to match their speed, or can you help adjust the vibe of the room and bring it to where you'd rather it be?

You can do this. Adjust your breath and slow it down today. You can do this with a simple exercise. Take 20 deep breaths down to your lower abdomen and work to slow your breathing with each exhale. With each breath, try to drop into a slower rhythm.

Once you've connected with this deeper place, step back into your day and observe your velocity as it shifts. Check the cadence of your voice and slow it down or speed it up as you deem fit. With a little practice you'll find that people are easy to nudge. You can bring peace and serenity to a room by first finding it within yourself and then helping spread it through the people around you. We're all like antennae that pick up vibes around us while *simultaneously* broadcasting. It's a two-way street that we're woefully unaware of, and it's led to immeasurable suffering.

Enough.

Today practice paying attention to how you feel around the people you interact with. How fast are they buzzing? Are they spinning or coming from a peaceful center? Do you need to walk away, or can you bring some positive influence to the party? Breathe down to your lower abdomen and calm your mind. Change the cadence of your voice and see what it does. Play with it and help bring more peace to the world around you.

It's time to recognize how influential you are, whether you're adding to the chaos or bringing it under control. Today you learn your central role in the entire universe, one human engagement at a time.

DAY 43

purchase decisions

How often do you stress about money? If you're like most people, the answer is probably too often. We live in a world where there's too much to buy and too little money to have it all. The mass-consumption economy is driving us into extinction, but we insist on having the latest things and keeping up with new fashion, tech, and whatever else is trending. It's exhausting.

Today let's do a little exercise. Most consumer-products companies have placed bets on our impulsive behavior. We tend to not think things through at the point of purchase and oftentimes end up going home with things we don't need. Advertising drives us to feel incomplete, and the countless items stacked up for sale in front of us all carry some promise of fulfillment. More often than not, we tend to fall for this and spend our hard-earned money on something we probably don't need. That money was time and life energy that you just sunk into yet another thing that isn't going to actually make you any happier.

Today's exercise is stopping time to cultivate mindfulness around what you buy. Whether it's in line at the coffee shop or checking out a cart of stuff online, you have agency in this. That impulsive moment of purchase has millions of dollars of psychological research behind it. The brands and advertisers need you to fall here, to go ahead and buy that thing.

Not today. Whenever facing a purchase decision, take 30 seconds and breathe down to your lower abdomen.

Then ask yourself:

- Do I really need this thing?
- Am I going to enjoy this after one week? One month? One year?
- Where will this thing end up when I'm finished with it? A landfill? In the ocean?
- Does this thing make the world a better, healthier place?
- Am I supporting slave labor or gender inequality by buying this?
- Do I *really* need this thing or not?

If you're okay with it, then fine—go ahead. Be honest with yourself and really get into this exercise though. You'll find that there's an unconscious tendency in most of us to spend money (time and energy) and buy things that add to the world's problems while not fulfilling the promise of making us truly happy.

What can you do today that actually sparks joy and drives change in yourself? Let's think about experiences versus things. What memorable experience can you have today that'll help enrich your life? Chances are, that doesn't cost anything. Go reward yourself with some real experience, and keep your cash in your pocket today.

DAY 44

chair time

Sitting is the new smoking. There's plenty of evidence to support this statement. Our bodies shut down after about 30 minutes of sitting: Our blood flow slows, our resting metabolic rate lowers, and our postural muscles start to fail as we collapse. We age faster, recover more slowly, and have less available energy to fuel our brains. After just half an hour! None of this is good.

Knowing this, today you're going to hold a stand-in for your life. Unless you're driving or flying, avoid any and all seats. If you're at a desk, prop up your computer with a box or move to a countertop for the day. If it's the weekend, avoid sedentary activities. Get creative and make it happen. At home, this means no sofa time. You can sit on the ground and stretch, but no chairs or sofas at all today.

This exercise will force you to look at how often you sit. This position has become our go-to for communication, meetings, work, eating, and even talking on the phone. Take those calls while pacing in your office. Eat at the kitchen counter, and avoid sitting even for meals today. This isn't a daily practice but an opportunity to learn something about yourself. Stay up and keep walking, pacing, doing lunges, or stretching.

One thing you'll notice is how different it feels. You may notice that your abdominal muscles are sore. It turns out they have to work to keep us upright when standing. Hello, future six-pack.

What happens when we break the habit of sitting daily is almost magical. We liberate ourselves from a physical rut, protect ourselves from the shutdown of our physiology, and become more alive and engaged. With more energy burning and creating a need for through-put in you, your muscles start to have greater capacity and your brain has more access to this boost in energy. The more efficiently you burn, the better your metabolism becomes. This throughput keeps you energized and doesn't store those calories as fat. This means more clarity, better mood, improved performance, and, frankly, *more time*. Yes, when you have more energy, you gain more time. You are a better version of yourself. You can do more in less time, and the wind drag of being tired or foggy goes away.

Do this practice all day and take note of how often you are accustomed to sitting each day. It'll surprise you to realize how many waking hours you spend with your body essentially shutting down. There's a chance you'll be a bit beat up by day's end, since there are lots of muscles that have gotten lazy over the years, but this should serve as an incentive to stand more often and build this into your life.

Wear good shoes, which will make today easier. Walking helps a lot versus standing around all day. The eventual goal is to increase the *movement* in your life, which will trigger all sorts of positive things. The sooner you can get used to staying in movement, the better off you'll be.

Does this mean never sit? Of course not. But think about how much of your life you've spent sitting, and see what happens if you take this one day to avoid it. Once you develop an appreciation for this practice, the times you do sit become intentional and conscious. You sit and you enjoy it once you've shifted the math and moved to a more active lifestyle.

DAY 45

enjoy this place

When we're young, we tend to encounter a new place and think, "Oh, I'll be back here." That seems to change with the passing years, and we come to a new orientation around space. We realize that the world is quite large and our time is limited. There's actually a pretty good chance that we'll never be back to that place. After all, lots of stars lined up to put us there in the first place, and all things being equal, odds are we'll want to see something new next time.

So what does that mean for today? If you find yourself passing through a new place, think to yourself that this may be the only time you get to experience it. It's a subtle shift in perspective but one that pulls a missing part of you back into your body. As if your very spirit is looking through your eyes and registering every shape, texture, color, and detail of the place you're in, there's something magical about reality when experienced with full presence.

Maybe today you have your usual routine: kids to school, off to the office, gym at lunch, and then reverse your way back to bed. That's fine, but what about taking a new route to the gym? Add the experience of a new place to your journey today. It doesn't have to be Tahiti or the pyramids. Maybe it's another street, where you experience a fantastic sycamore tree. That's new, and that's beautiful.

Wherever you go, take the awareness of this practice with you today. After all, you can be hit by a bus, drowned in a tsunami, or crushed by a meteor. These things happen. Granted, they don't happen often, but let's take a lesson from our elderly friends. Death is around the corner for all of us, and today may well be your last. Knowing that, how would you look at the world differently? Would you mindlessly jam through this place, or would you stop to smell the roses?

That's the difference. Today is to be savored. This place is sacred. This time is special. There's magic all around us, but we neglect to slow down and notice it, because we're not actually here. We typically function in some mental realm of stress mixed with anticipation of future events and regrets over past ones. We may be standing here, but nobody's home.

Today you practice countering that tendency. Pull it in and pay attention to where you are. Practice telling yourself that you may never see this place again, so take a moment to savor it. Pull in the sights, sounds, textures, and the quality of light. In one hour, this place will look different. This moment in time and space is unique. When we come to that realization and actually live by it, we stop time and drink from infinity.

Stop and appreciate the majesty all around you.

DAY 46

pulling weeds in your life garden

When is the last time you looked at your Life Garden and pulled some weeds? Once you've identified the main plants that you want to grow and nurture, you need to turn your eyes to the other items that are also growing there. Why? Because they're pulling off vital water and nutrients and may be blocking sunlight to the plants you choose.

Think about this in the context of your life today. What are the main plants you want to nourish? Are those the ones that currently get the most resources? For many of us, the weeds have begun to take over the garden because they are more demanding, more aggressive, and are often masquerading as something important. Family, career, health, good friends, and travel may be on top of your list of real plants. How much time do you need to devote to those items in order to take good care of them, and what will it take to keep them in balance? Oftentimes, we find that maintaining the balance of the main items is hard enough. So then what else is in the garden that doesn't belong?

Look through the filter of your Life Garden and see if what is growing is relevant to one of your main plants. If not, then it's a weed. Pluck and move on. Maybe an old high school friend keeps pressing to hang out "for old times' sake." You have nothing in common and have enough on your plate, but for some reason you feel obliged to part with your valuable time to hang with him. Is this a weed?

Perhaps you're wrapped up in a book that isn't too interesting but you keep going because you don't want to be a quitter. It may be time to put it down and pick up another that enriches your life.

You may find that you're behind on sleep but are staying up later than you should, trying to binge-watch a new TV series. Is this really that important to you?

There needs to be some time for reflection and contemplation in your day today. We often don't know how to pull those weeds to eradicate them for good. Sometimes we may even be reluctant to do it. We grow attached to certain things. They've grown up strong and resemble the other big plants, so we feel they need to stay. They do not. Consider everything objectively and be mindful of weeds that resemble plants.

Get brutal today. Pull out the clippers (or the wood chipper) and start cutting back the leaves and stems of the weeds. You may need to do this until you can grab them by the stalk and pull the root out. You may even need a mental or emotional shovel for this work. Lay waste to everything, and be honest about what you see in your garden. Use broad strokes and have items earn their way back in. The challenge is that you've been watering several weeds for years and they've grown strong and look like they fit in.

Pull them out. Today you get clarity and focus by clearing anything that drains you of life force, which isn't on your plan. Is it in your Life Garden or not? That's the question. If not, then get to work.

DAY 47

music

"Music is the space between the notes." Have you ever heard this saying?

It is a beautiful illustration of a Taoist principle of emptiness. The notes themselves would drive us crazy if there were no reprieve between them. However, that's how we insist on living our lives.

Today we learn to stop time by riding with music. Pick a track you particularly love and make some space to quietly sit with it. My favorite song for this practice is "Adagio" by Remo Giazotto, often attributed to Albinoni. There are many versions, so find one you like, or again, go to your favorite piece.

Take one pass and simply listen to the song of your choice (ideally an instrumental track). This is not a time for multitasking; you shouldn't also be on your phone or doing a chore. On the next pass, see if you can sync your breathing with the cadence of the song. Does it speed up in places and slow down in others? How long do some of the silent moments linger? Pay attention to the tempo and see if you can sense a shift in it.

If you are musically oriented, you may already do this naturally. If not, this may take a few passes to train your ear. Know that it is not only about hearing but also about perceiving. How does it make you feel? What mood does it elicit? How can you change your physical being to sync to it? Slow down and *perceive* the music.

Now go back to the original saying and reflect upon it: "Music is the space between the notes."

Where in your life do you need to pause between notes? What subtle spacing can you put in your day to make things more beautiful? Maybe you take 15 minutes at lunch to walk around the office building or outside. Maybe you gather yourself at the day's end before getting into the car. Maybe you create space to move away from your desk and take some regular breaks throughout your day. These are choices for you to make.

What spacing would make your life's song more beautiful? If you notice, the music doesn't pause for very long and gets the intended effect. The key is to *fully stop* and tap into emptiness when you do. A partial pause doesn't get the same effect, as it'll sound like noise in the background.

Where can you embed momentary silence in your life today? Go back and listen to your song and get a feel for its cadence once again. Learn to master this and you'll live life with beauty and grace.

DAY 48

quality time with your family

One of the most common things we hear from people on their deathbeds is that they wish they would have spent more time with their family and loved ones. At the end of the show, nobody is thinking about their work woes, dramas, or superficial friends. They are often regretful for not having spent quality time with family when it counted. This may mean being there at the delicious age when our baby starts to walk or maybe when it's time to learn how to climb a tree. Perhaps we need to be there for our spouse when she loses a parent or when she gets sick. Oftentimes, families break apart when something heavy happens and the other person is simply not emotionally available for them.

Where are you not spending the adequate amount of time? Is it with your spouse, kids, parents, pets, or cousins? We have people in our lives who love us and matter to us. To many of them, it can be perceived that we are voting with our time. In the case of a teenager, maybe she sees how absorbed you are in your career, hobbies, sports, or social circle. She wants to come home and talk to you about something that's bothering her, but you don't get the cue. Two years later she's smoking pot and off in a challenging direction. This happens.

Perhaps your spouse is having a hard time with a newly emptied nest and your "get over it" attitude isn't serving her needs. There's a wedge forming in your relationship that can't be mended once it snaps. Countless marriages end this way. Can you pull over from life's superhighway and dedicate some time to talk, hike, travel, or just listen? On a practical level, that divorce will take thousands of hours of lawyer and court time, which costs a fortune. That fortune is banked-up time in the form of money. It'll cost more money in a settlement, and then there's the joint custody, awkward family dinners, dealing with the kids, and the hours of swiping left or right on some dumb dating app you'd rather not be on. Think about the thousands of painful hours that will follow a broken marriage. Isn't it worth a few well-spent hours with your beloved?

Think about where you may be out of balance with your family. Are you due for a weekend with your daughter, or has it been a month since you've visited your folks? They need you. They love you. Don't let life's endless stream of distractions carry you down the white water of chaos into a life filled with regret. You'll end up spending more time thinking about your kids' problems and juggling custody issues if you drop the ball anyhow. The guilt that comes when a parent dies is enormous when we know we weren't available to spend quality time with them before they passed. Certain things need to be said. These things take time, and Grandpa is in a much slower time zone than you. That's cool. Slow your roll and hang with him. Drink some tea and let him speak his mind and open his heart to you. When he's gone, those unsaid items become daggers of remorse that you drag around with you for years.

Some quality time spent doing the right thing today will save time, grief, and remorse later on.

Make that call. Our life's circumstances are all so different, but your practice today should be in carving out a regular time you can consistently book with your family. Dinner is ideal, but take what you can get. Find the time and block it off. Make sure there's buy-in among all family members, and establish this time block as a regular, recurring event. Hold the line and you'll reap the benefits.

DAY 49

time and technology

Technology is something we created to help us save time and energy. From the earlier flints that bought us time away from banging rocks together to the phone in your pocket that can do so much, these human-made tools at our disposal are supposed to add convenience, leisure, and time to our lives.

Today take a look at how you use your technology. Is it actually saving you time to do what you want for yourself or not? For some, it helps enhance productivity, which allows them to do more and more work. That may be fine if you are banking the money and buying time away to recover, enjoy, and savor life. If not, then you're a dying hamster.

For too many of us, these time-saving devices have themselves become time sucks. Getting vital information passed along a telegraph was a powerful tool for civilization. Today we pepper our friends with GIFs and emojis out of boredom. It is clutter. Countless hours per week of looking at other people's lives on social media isn't the best use of your time (or that device), but even when we're genuinely trying to get work done, our devices can make it hard. Constant alerts, reminders, and notifications can pull us out of what we're doing. Looking up one relevant piece of information can too quickly suck us down a rabbit hole of distractions.

What's your technology doing for you? Is it a time-saving tool in your life, or has it become a distraction? Look at all the things you say you want to be doing for yourself and see where the time suck is. Oftentimes, our technology has outgrown its functional utility and is now out of line. The tools are meant to serve you, not the other way around.

Another consideration here is energy. Nature is imbued with a delicious symphony of vibrations and energies. From pollinating flowers to majestic, tall trees, there's an energy in the natural environment that recharges us and makes us feel whole. Electronics are the opposite of that. They run currents on our laps or by our heads that are edgy and intense. Holding a 2.4 gigahertz phone up to your head sends powerful waves through your brain that are often disruptive. Electronics put off fast waves that our bodies are unaccustomed to. The science on this is still shaky, but why take a chance? Trees, on the other hand, flow nice and slowly. They vibrate right around the alpha wave pattern of our brains. This is the brain state that most closely resembles meditation.

Our technology is here to stay, and your challenge today is to negotiate a healthier balance with it. Just for today turn off the alerts. Make a list on paper of what you need to accomplish today, and focus on getting through it. Put your phone in airplane mode and disable the Internet from your computer. Get your work done and then give your eyes and ears a rest. Bask in sunlight and not the backlight of your laptop. You'll notice an enormous difference if you pay attention to this.

DAY 50

setting rituals

Rituals used to be a big part of our lives. Whether they were daily prayers, weekly dinners, religious festivals, or rites of passage, they have been ingrained in our psyche since the dawn of humanity.

Today let's look at any rituals you observe in your life. What are they, and why do you do them? Do you watch the news on TV during breakfast? Do you check social media on the toilet? Are you going through the motions, or are you plugged into the spirit of the activity? So many of the things we do in modern times come from ancient origins. *They used to mean something.* They helped set the tempo of life and were often designed to help us *remember* where we came from. Religious rituals were set to help us keep connected with our source or maybe to practice gratitude.

What are you doing in life that helps you stop time and connect with something meaningful? Can you be better at it? Maybe you can reconnect with the spirit of the ritual and take it more seriously. Maybe you can research its origin and connect with it better. It may be that you find yourself disconnected with this activity and bored—that's fine. There are plenty of other rituals you can adopt.

The point is to find something that serves you and allow it to be an anchor in your life. If you don't connect with it, then it isn't serving its intended purpose. Don't waste time. Find another activity or practice that you can vibe with.

Here are some examples of rituals you may adopt. Pick one or two as your gong item for today and give them a try. Chances are, you'll like some of your new habits.

- **Morning gratitude.** Before you get out of bed, run through five things you're grateful for today.
- **Mealtime prayer.** Give thanks for the meal in front of you and take a moment to bless it.
- **Lunchtime meditation or prayer.** Take a few seconds to slow down and allow for your body to receive nourishment.
- **Evening candlelight sit.** Spend a few minutes across from a candle and let it cleanse your energy.
- **Nighttime stretch.** Before bed, spend a few minutes relaxing into your body and melting into the floor.
- **Winter hibernation.** Each winter, take a week off from work to relax and catch your breath.

These are just a few rituals you can think about. The questions are, what do you need, and how can you assemble a practice in your life that'll help you remember and reconnect?

Rituals create structure, and this helps break up the day. Time can get away from us when we don't set trip wires during the day to stop the craziness and catch our breath.

Today think through your existing rituals and make sure they are serving you. Find a way to connect with what you need, and make a plan to build healthier practices into your life.

DAY 51

stopping time to make love

Having sex and making love are not always the same. Our culture has driven the sensuality of our lovemaking experience and reduced it to a get-some-pleasure and release-some-tension pit stop. Sure, an occasional quickie can be great, but when's the last time you slowed down your sexual experience and turned the night into an event?

Making love requires slowing time. It means settling into the parasympathetic nervous system, which is a more relaxed state. This is where we heal, digest, recover, and, yes, get into the *sensuality of our sexuality*. This is often easier for females than males (yes, a gross generalization), but we're all capable of doing this.

Here's the big secret of tantra: Human sensuality is actually driven by the female (yin) energy. Now, if you're in a same-sex relationship, this doesn't exclude you. It simply means to follow the more yin, or passive, energy curve, and allow it to open and guide you into the experience.

We don't *do* sleep, and we can't really *do* orgasms. Sure, we can hyperexcite the nerves and take it over the top, but that's not the energy we're talking about today. Today we relax into the experience and *allow* for the space to open up.

For many people, this means setting the stage. Candles, low light, soft music, and maybe a bottle of wine are all nice to set the mood. It's important to create a distraction-free space where you can enjoy some time together and go there. No phones!

It may mean waiting till the kids are asleep. That's fine, but then get to it! Don't go watching 3 hours of TV before heading upstairs to also squeeze this in. That totally misses the point. The practice is to make an evening (or a good afternoon) of it. Get into that room, set the mood, and block off the time to relax into an experience of lovemaking.

All too often, our goal-oriented minds spill over into the bedroom, and we have a get-it-done mentality where it's inappropriate. Not here, not in the bedroom. If your partner has an issue with this, maybe play a single- or double-sided no-orgasm game. Practice hanging out and enjoying a sensual space without the sudden exit of climax. If you're the type who can have multiple orgasms and stay in that space, well, good for you (today's lesson is probably not a newsflash either).

Relax.

Sink.

Breathe together to your lower abdomen and connect up at the lower dantian (three fingers below your navel). Syncing your breathing will do this. From there, *feel* how the energy rises up the spine, and stay with this energy. Relax into it. Let it guide and illuminate your inner universe.

Don't go for climax.

Instead, today's lesson is to relax into the space you've co-created and savor it. With some practice, this will give you a whole new perspective on *stopping time*.

DAY 52

phone time

When is the last time you audited how much time you spend on your phone? Are you on calls all day? Unless you're billing by the hour and that's how your job works, chances are you're losing precious time being inefficient. Today let's try something new.

At work, look at any calls that are on your calendar and see if you could cut them in half. Say there's a 30-minute call scheduled: Can you get off in 15? How about 25? You needn't be rude, just nice and to the point. Work on giving them all of your attention, start with some nice pleasantry, and then jump in. Hammer through whatever you need to discuss and see if you can end the call a little early without causing any drama.

Here's the deal: The person on the other side also has a crazy, busy life, and she probably won't mind (as long as you've covered what you need).

Now, what do you do with the extra time? How about all the things you've been *meaning to do*? Today's exercise is to reabsorb any and all time you save and reinvest it in *yourself*. If you have 5 extra minutes, then you can do some stretching. Have 10 minutes? Do five sets of 10 exercises for a quick, whole-body workout. Are you sleep-deprived? Set a timer and close your eyes for 10 minutes.

The point is that you have reabsorbed valuable time that can be reinvested in an area of life that needs it.

What about social calls? Maybe you call Mom on your drive home. Does it serve you and nourish your soul? Cool, then keep it. But what about all the other social calls? Can you text? Can you cut them short and find something more nourishing to do with your time? Chances are the answer is a resounding *yes*.

This isn't about cutting off the world and becoming a hermit. It's about shaving off a few minutes here and there and *using that time* to do something that nourishes you. Ask your body what it needs and then use that time for some self-care. Maybe you change a regular check-in call with a friend into a weekly hike: win-win!

Once you discover that your world won't come to a screeching halt over this, you can then look at your calendar and make more adjustments. Trim your standard 60-minute calls to 30 or 30-minute calls to 15. This alone can change your life.

Here's the trick though: Unless you *invest* the newly found time into something that supports your health and sanity, your schedule will simply fill up with more items. This may be a great way to up your efficiency at work, but it can also crush your soul if you don't take the time (or at least some of it) for yourself!

DAY 53

relax the back of your neck

We hold a tremendous amount of tension in our necks, especially in the occiput, right in the middle at the base of the skull. With bad posture, too much sitting, a stagnant lifestyle, and abundant stress levels, lots of energy gets stuck in the back of the neck. We can feel the tension. It radiates into our head or wraps into a scowl or frown on our face. It is uncool.

Today we're going to lean into this and do something about it.

Find a place to lie down flat on your back—anywhere is fine as long as you won't be disturbed for 5 minutes. Grab a book, binder, or yoga block if you have one. You need a firm pillow, basically something without any give that isn't too big; aim for 1 to 3 inches high.

Lie down with the object as your pillow, placed directly at the base of the skull, and close your eyes. Start breathing slowly down to your lower abdomen for a minute or so. Relax and sink.

Now begin to bring your awareness to the back of your neck. Feel the firm pillow and where it is contacting the base of your skull. Melt into it a bit. Breathe and relax and let your head get heavy.

Now slowly rotate your head from left to right and back while breathing slowly. Do this for about a minute, gently rolling from side to side and letting your neck relax.

Now come back to the center and breathe deeply. Again, feel whatever tension is there and *melt* into your rigid pillow. Let's take a couple more minutes here.

Relax the muscles of your face: your forehead, your jaw, around your eyes. Relax your mouth, ears, nose, brows. Sink deeper and relax your head and neck fully. Sink. Breathe deeply and sink. Take a minute or so when you're ready to slowly open your eyes, rotate from side to side again, and gently roll up and get back into your day. How do you feel?

The back of the neck is an energy superhighway where lots of our stuck *qi* (energy) builds up. In fact, time compression is often reflected in this part of the anatomy. Releasing it helps relax the brain and bring us back into the present moment. All of those instances where you got pulled into a faster time than you were comfortable with can be found reflected here.

It's a great place to go to press reset and become present. Learning to relax the back of the neck is a powerful way to stop time and drop deeply into the present. It's where you can flush out past time pollution and clear the decks for a fresh restart to your day.

DAY 54

social media day off

Today we're going to try to reclaim some valuable time back into your life. We've become so accustomed to checking our phones every day that we are probably unaware of how much it can add up. Let's take some time off nonessential tasks on your phone (or computer) and see exactly how much mental energy and time you get back.

For those of you already clutching your phones, I get it: Social media is a way to feel connected to your world and in the loop. But checking it can become a social tick that completely removes you from the world around you, and it's time to break the habit. So what's on the media blackout list?

- Any and all social media—don't look at it or open any apps
- The news
- Your pictures or videos
- Chat apps where you banter with your friends

Tell your friends you'll be cut off from your phone today, and keep to this exercise. You'll likely find yourself reaching for your phone at several occasions throughout the day. This is when you remember to disengage and avoid going there.

Let's go through some common examples of times you're likely to check your phone:

- Waiting for an elevator
- In an elevator

- In line at a coffee shop
- On the toilet
- At a red light
- In the subway
- Waiting for your lunch to arrive
- In bed
- On the sofa
- Waiting for food to warm up
- In between calls
- During calls

Does any of this sound familiar to you? It's gotten out of hand. We're constantly checking our phones during any downtime. We've become unconscious of it, and the challenge is in reclaiming some of this time.

We can't complain about the scarcity of a resource that we squander every day. Take it back. Savor it, and enjoy the spaciousness of the free time you would have lost to your phone today.

Whenever you catch yourself wanting to go there, stop yourself and take a few breaths down to your lower abdomen. Check in with your body and ask what it needs. Are you reaching for your phone because there's information that you urgently need or because you're not used to being alone with your thoughts? Are you using social media to benefit your life, or is it more of a security blanket? Perhaps a quick stretch, some water, some people watching, or just standing there is the answer. The point is, there are millions of micromoments that go down the abyss of this modern time suck, and it is on you to pull them back.

DAY 55

five breaths for you

Today we're going to play a little game. Set a timer for every 30 minutes. Whenever your timer pings, stop what you're doing and simply take five deep breaths down to your lower abdomen. It's a simple practice that can go a long way (and you're going to be breathing anyway, so seriously don't cheat). Remember to follow through and do it every time your timer goes off, and see what you feel like throughout your day. The practice is easy. Focus on slowing the inhale and holding for a second at the top of the breath. Then make a long, deep exhale flow out smoothly and hold for a moment at the bottom of your empty breath. Do this mindfully five times and then go back to your day. The alarm will bring you back when it's time.

The first few times may not spark any huge shifts in you. That's normal. Keep with it. As you train your body and mind to press pause and nourish your breath regularly, something starts to shift. It may take the greater part of the day, but it'll eventually happen.

We're so used to operating under duress that we don't remember what it's like to feel at peace anymore. We've grown accustomed to the wound-up energy of stress. It somehow defines us and has worked its way into our personal narrative. Our scattered attention leads to scattered energy that dissipates into the universe. No wonder we feel so tired all the time.

"I'm so damned busy I don't even have time to pee . . . hahaha."

Nope. That's not funny; that's insane. We've had enough of that.

Taking five breaths for yourself is a quick remedy to reset this rhythm. The key is to make the breaths count. Banging through five quick breaths as a throwaway gesture is *exactly* the energy we're working to correct. It may take 10 to 15 seconds longer to breathe properly. But what's that in the grand scheme of things? Nothing. The challenge is not the time. It is the whole emotional world that's wrapped up in the perception of time compression. That consciousness doesn't want to allow for a change of tempo. Why?

Because that'll open us up to the possibility that the freight train we're on is vulnerable. Think of an alcoholic who needs to keep drinking after lunch so she doesn't feel the crash. That's how we behave with stressed time. Somehow we've trained ourselves to think it's acceptable to push through it, even when that means doing a less-than-optimal job at work, missing the gym, staying cranky for our drive, and often being a jerk to our family. Remind me again how that's the better option than slowing down for 10 minutes per day?

Today you press pause twice per hour. Take the five breaths and use them as a focal point to gather your attention and focus your mind. Feel them throughout your body and use them to become aware of your whole self for a few seconds. Taking control of your mind's velocity and quickly checking in is a powerful practice that starts with simplicity and begets simplicity.

What if the solutions to your complicated problems were not so complicated? What if they were as simple as slowing down so you could think more clearly and come from a balanced place?

Today you'll discover much about yourself.

DAY 56

progressive relaxation

Let's take a deep dive into a relaxed state today. This practice is common in most Asian meditation traditions and is also used in modern hypnotherapy. You may not have allowed yourself to go here in some time. It'll feel like a homecoming for some and an odd foreign land for others. Trust the process and let's sink deep into a progressive relaxation.

You'll want to read through this chapter and then go find a comfortable place to lie down for about 15 minutes. Make sure you'll be left alone and feel safe there. Once you've read this, go to your room and perform it. Set a timer to go off 5 minutes before you're finished so you can come out of it gracefully. For example, if you can allot 20 minutes, set your timer for 15 so you have 5 minutes to come back to the room.

HERE'S THE PRACTICE

- Lie down in a comfortable position.
- Take a few breaths down to your lower abdomen and relax into the ground. Sink.
- Now let's start with your head.
  - Feel the top of your head, and as your mind's eye comes to awareness of this region, tell this area to relax.
  - Feel it getting heavier and sinking into the ground.
- From the top of the head, start moving down your face and relaxing everything progressively.

- Relax your forehead, eyes, ears, nose, cheeks, teeth, and chin.
- Relax the back of your head and nape of your neck.
- Relax your entire head. Let it get heavy and sink into the ground.
- Keep moving down the body.
  - Relax your neck, throat, shoulders, and down your arms to your fingertips.
  - Relax your chest, ribs, sternum, and upper back.
  - Relax your abdomen, all of your internal organs, mid back, and low back.
  - Relax your pelvis, hips, genitals, and sacrum.
- Move down both legs, relaxing everything as you descend . . . slowly.
  - Relax your knees, shins, calves, and down to your ankles.
  - Relax your feet, every little bone, all the way down to your toes.
- Feel your whole body in a state of relaxation.
- Scan from top to bottom and bottom to top and see if there's any tension left. Move your mind's eye to this part and simply tell it to relax.

Once you're in this state, hang here and let everything sink farther into the ground. Breathe deeply and continue to scan your body for tension. Soften the places you find tension and continue to relax into the ground.

WHEN YOUR TIMER GOES OFF

Slowly start to come back to the room. Begin by visualizing a warm, white light coming up into your feet. This white light invigorates and brings energy to anything it touches. Have the light slowly work up your body in reverse order of how you relaxed it. Have it work all the way up to the top of your head. Stay there and breathe deeply as the white light awakens every cell of your body. See the brightness in your forehead once it's all the way up there.

When ready, slowly open your eyes, wiggle your toes, roll to one side, and come back to the room. It didn't take too much time out of your day, but where did you just go?

DAY 57

seasons

Today we're going to stop and take stock of where we stand in earth time. What does that mean? Well, what season is it? Where are you currently in nature's cycle? Are the leaves sprouting or falling? Is it hot or cold? What's happening outside?

Our ancestors were acutely aware of the seasons because their life depended on it. Whether it was the movement of herds or the right time to plant or harvest, it mattered—it was life and death. Nowadays, we live in air conditioning and drive around in bubbles, oblivious to the changing energies of the natural world all around us. But not today!

Step outside for a few minutes today and take stock of the climate. Look at the trees all around you and notice the quality of the air. How does it feel? Are the natural energies around you in decline or are they rising? Where is the movement of life? Take a few breaths to your lower abdomen and sync up with the outside world. Harmonize with it. If it's cold, grab a sweater; you'll survive 5 minutes.

Getting in sync with the flavor of nature is a big part of our being. It aligns our energy with that of the big world all around us; it calibrates us to the natural reality in which we dwell.

When's the last time you did this?

Computer screens, news from far-off lands, and app updates inundate our days now when, just a few hundred years ago, we'd sit on the porch and talk about the weather. Why? Because it is *real* and it actually relates to us. It affects our moods, our hormone secretions, our metabolic rate, and our wake-sleep cycles. It influences us in ways we're just beginning to understand scientifically.

The moral of the story: Get attuned with where you stand in nature and harmonize with the flow of this season. The sun makes us happy and boosts our immune system. Plants secrete odors in the spring that signal hormonal changes in us.

It is time to take stock of where you stand in time this season. Take several deep breaths and notice the sights, colors, sounds, smells, breeze, and movement of animals. This will tune you into the real time that the natural world is dwelling in all around you. It'll connect you with the earth and the life force that permeates all of nature.

This is home. This is now.

Today you will spend some time returning to it by accessing the season in which you're living right now.

DAY 58

reactive decisions

How often do you need to make big life decisions? Usually they don't come too often in life, certainly not every day. Now, sure you can say, "I decided not to quit my job today," but that's a daily frustration. A career change, divorce, decision to have a kid, decision to move to a far-off town—these are all big life decisions. Think back to the major life decisions you've made in the past decade. You can usually count them on a hand or two. Now recall whether you were of sound mind and body when you made those decisions. Were they made under careful deliberation? Did you weigh out the pros and cons and spend enough time in thought and counsel over each decision? If so, then good for you.

Unfortunately, many big life decisions come under duress. We're totally stressed out and some circumstance snaps us into another reality. This may have been a powerful course correction to put us on the path we're supposed to be on, or it may turn out to be the worst decision we've ever made. How do your decisions feel?

Think through your history of big decisions today and give a close examination to the ones that came under the gun. What could you have done differently had you been calm and collected? If you were able to breathe deeply to your core and focus your energy on staying in the moment, would you have acted the same way? What might your life look like had you been better prepared for the situation?

This isn't an exercise in reloading old regrets as much as one designed to lay a better path for you in the future. There are more big life decisions coming your way, and you can carry wisdom from your past into the circumstances of the future. The only way you can do that though is to *be calm and present when the moment comes*. That's where we draw upon wisdom. It comes from the peaceful stillness of a gathered soul. If you feel yourself reacting from a place of panic, anger, fear, or haste, take a step outside the moment and see it for what it is.

Reflecting on this today, you can prepare your consciousness for the next round by understanding the magnitude of a hasty decision. Next time, remember today's practice and take a deep breath. Slow down and think of the past decisions made in haste. Diffuse your emotions so that you can act from a place of calm rather than a place of panic. There usually isn't a gun to our head in these moments. We tilt our hands before we need to.

Walk away from an inciting incident. Take a night or few to sleep on it. Phone a friend. There are numerous smart things you can do before pulling the trigger on something you can't easily take back. Slow down and step out of that timeline and into one that'll get you the best outcome. Next time, be ready.

DAY 59

sweating

We've all heard that sweating is good for us. Sure, it helps detoxify the body, move the lymph system, and keep fluids circulating. That's great, but today there's another facet to this that we're going to explore that has to do with *clearing the past*.

What's stored in your body tissue is yesterday's gunk. Your liver may have been too tired to clear it. Maybe you've exposed yourself to one of the gazillion toxins in our environment that the body doesn't know how to purge. Perhaps you've ingested a heavy metal that has bound to your fat cells. These things tend to hang around and drag us down—it feels like running with weights on our ankles.

Now imagine what life would feel like without such a burden. Imagine how you would feel if yesterday's challenges didn't saddle you now. That's why you should want to sweat.

Think of sweating as a river that flows through you. It purges and cleans out the gunk from upstream and makes for a healthier environment. If the past (in the form of toxic thoughts, chemical, foods, or energies) has no outlet, then it stays in your system and negatively impacts your present day. A healthy body has a constant flow of water moving through it, and because of our physiology, the skin is an important place where this happens.

The natural ways to move water through the body are urine, feces, and sweat. All three need to do their part, and each has its place. The liver predominantly pulls the toxins from the blood and moves them out through the intestines, and that's why having regular bowel movements is important. This doesn't mean that the other channels don't count. We also detoxify through our skin, but most of us hardly sweat on an average day. That's like plugging up a toilet and wondering why the room stinks. This is a major pathway we have used for millennia to clear out the junk.

You need to sweat *daily,* and today's the day you start. Find an exercise that will get you worked up, and do it until you're profusely sweating. A sauna can work, but exercise also has other potent benefits, so make that your gold standard.

Think of a river that doesn't flow. It gunks up and turns green. A stopped river is a sick river. Is that happening to you right now?

This river flowing through time is alive and well in your body. You're never looking at the same river, and your body is in a constant state of flux.

Unlock the flow and let yesterday's challenges move on through you.

DAY 60

time in the sun

The sun's gotten a bad rap lately. We're all told that UV exposure leads to skin cancer, and we've been so bombarded with messages about the dangers of tanning that many of us have been shocked into staying indoors or lathering on sunscreen under a silly hat. Of course, too much UV exposure can cause problems, but we're also facing a baby-bathwater scenario here. We need the sunlight to trigger vitamin D synthesis. We need full-spectrum light to balance our neurotransmitters, and we probably need dozens of other things the sun does that science has yet to discover. Our bodies are made to spend a healthy amount of time in the sun, and we need to make a concerted and careful effort to be outdoors more so that we can reap those benefits.

Today, regardless of the season or temperature, try to get some time outside. Don't freeze to death or scorch yourself, but get out under an open sky and let the sun's rays shower down on you. Cloudy? It's better than nothing, and you're still getting many of the benefits.

Okay, so just stand there?

No—drink. *Drink light.*

This is a powerful practice that we've forgotten in modern times. Plants take sunlight and photosynthesize energy. This is one of the miracles of life and has allowed for us to grow through the food chain.

Today drink sunlight like a plant. Stand out there and drink it through every pore on your body. Close your eyes and visualize the sun's rays coming into your body through every cell. Drive it deep down into the core of your being with every inhale, and then allow it to dissipate throughout your body on the exhale.

Spend several breaths here, basking and drinking. Expose your skin to the elements as much as is comfortable. It's easier with direct sunlight, but hey, take what you can get. With some practice, you'll find this practice incredibly rejuvenating. In fact, you may even be able to find ancient plant DNA in the depths of your consciousness, which can unlock some interesting skills. People who learn this practice and do it regularly get good at energizing their entire body, mind, and soul with sunlight.

Can you use some of that?

Great. The power source of all life on this planet is right there above you. Maybe it is time to connect with it and rekindle the inner fire that its rays can spark within you. Drink light.

DAY 61

teatime

There's a reason why teatime is taken so seriously in a number of cultures. It helps pace out the day. Somehow in the United States, we've become accustomed to pushing all day without any real breaks. Even during lunch, we scarf down some food so we can pick up the dry cleaning, run to the bank, and make a couple calls. It's gotten crazy.

Traditional cultures always padded the day with certain rituals that helped take the edge off. This helped people settle down, take a deep breath, and enjoy some pleasant conversation with the foot off the gas pedal.

When's the last time you did this in your life? Do you run your days like a maniac who can't stop or else you'll collapse? How sustainable is that? The point is to create a ritual around teatime that can serve as *sanity's anchor* in your life. Smokers take breaks all the time. Why shouldn't you?

Let's take a few minutes today and get a cup of tea. Put on a pot if you have the opportunity. It can be an herbal tea if you're sensitive to caffeine or if it's after 2 p.m. Find a time during your day that's a good hour before you are overwhelmed and too beat up. At that point you'll be thinking about wine and it'll be too late for tea. Teatime is designed to intercept that and help you blow off some steam, literally, before there's a dangerous amount of pressure built up in your system.

This ritual works because tea is not something you can drink in a rush. It takes time to brew and time to steep, and it is too hot to drink quickly. I recommend finding a wide-mouthed cup that you can hold in both hands and sip from slowly, and take some time to breathe in the steam. Ideally, you have one around midmorning and another in the midafternoon. This breaks the day up nicely and gives you chunks of time for productivity and little breaks that allow you to hit reset.

You needn't change your whole life around this, but take today as an experiment. Take two mini tea breaks during the day when you spend 10 to 15 minutes sipping the tea of your choice and relaxing, whether alone or with someone who won't talk about stressful work stuff.

It may take a few days to get used to this, but you'll soon find solace in the ritual and, remarkably, learn that your productivity will likely go up. Look at the British. They led the world in commerce and had the greatest empire the world had ever seen. They took the time for tea. Perhaps there's some wisdom we could glean from them.

See how you feel. If you like it, you can work to build a ritual like this into your life and see where that takes you.

You have plenty of time. The allocation is the issue. Taking some quality time for yourself makes the work time less taxing. When you're less taxed, you exert less energy and therefore feel better and are more productive. The math is simple. Don't fall for the American "you can rest when you're dead" mentality. That's killing everyone, including planet Earth. Today let's slow our roll and sip some tea.

Enjoy life: what a novel concept!

DAY 62

time by a fire

Today you need to find a fire. A gas one is fine, but the ideal would be a good, old-fashioned, wood-burning fire. Prepare to get comfortable and spend some time with it this evening.

Fire is an amazing thing that we tend not to contemplate. It is the release of energy from a material base that is unfolding in front of our eyes. That wood (or natural gas) is being brought to a state of hyper-excitability wherein the energy between the molecular bonds is released as heat. That energy was stored long ago—in the case of natural gas, probably very long ago.

So what you're doing is looking back into time. You're peering into a window of life energy that's been trapped in some material form that is now being released back to the atmosphere. It isn't static either. Like looking at a flowing river, the flame is constantly being formed anew, with fresh material combusting.

Sit down in front of your fire and contemplate its timelessness. Peer into the flame and look back into time. You are watching ancient energy coming at you, trapped energy from the sun that was brought into chemical bonds by some plant life and sequestered in carbon many years ago. This is therefore sunlight from a day on earth long ago.

How does the flame make you feel? The ancient Zoroastrians used fire to cleanse their own energy and purify their souls. They'd jump over it for holidays and sit by it with the conscious agreement that the fire was meant to cleanse their impurities.

This evening's practice is to settle down next to your fire and let yourself bathe in its light. Let the energy of the fire purify your thoughts, feelings, and mood as you sit there. Listen to the sound of the flame. Settle into it.

Once you've spent some time at this in front of a wood fire, you'll notice a powerful shift in cadence. Things heat up and get fast and furious with the addition of a new log, and then the quality of emission starts to settle and slow. If you wait too long, it goes out. The flames turn to red embers and fade.

Where are you with how you burn in life? Do you need to add new logs all day to keep the bonfire of your life going, or are you struggling to find wood to ignite? How is your flame burning, and what adjustments can you make to find a better burn rate? These are questions only you can answer and may require some serious thought. Let the actual fire in front of you serve as a mentor and guide your consciousness. Settle into the relaxed state it induces and let the energy it emits clear your mind. That's where the good ideas come from anyhow. Clear the deck and let inspiration come to you from a pure state. When there, think about your own fire and how you may adjust it to better serve your needs.

DAY 63

time and light

Time is tied to the quality of light we're experiencing. We've created a way to track our days by the movement of the sun and the tilt of our planet. This gives us the time of day and the seasons and is all related to the beams of photons coming our way from above.

Our perception of time is intimately tied to the amount of light in our environment. It helps cue our pineal gland to signal a slowdown for the day. We've been living by this mechanism for millions of years, and the past century has challenged this circuitry with an overabundance of light.

When you get out of the house early in the morning, take note of the velocity of the time signature all around you. It is slow. Things are beginning to stir. Birds may be starting to chirp, and there may be some distant car sounds starting to rev up. It is still peaceful and slow. Take a few deep breaths through your nostrils. Observe what's around you, and be barefoot if you can.

As the sun comes up, time begins to quicken. We start to move faster, and the world starts to buzz. In fact, the world keeps picking up steam and going well into the afternoon hours, but then the arc starts to drop. We look to going home and slowing down again. As the light begins to diminish, we are signaled to slow down and take our foot off the gas pedal.

At least, that's in an ideal universe. Regardless of where you live, the mornings are still relatively mellow and quiet. People slowly start to stir and get going, but we can experience some relative calm if we get up early enough. The challenge today is often in the evening hours, when, after the sun has gone down, we have access to plenty of light from our houses, devices, and TVs. This can keep us up far beyond the natural rhythm our bodies have evolved to be synced with.

See what happens when you play with these rhythms. Get out into the sun at noon and absorb some rays as well. How does that feel? Can you sense the difference in the quality of time? You should.

Today learn the difference in how you feel as the light around you begins to shift. The big swings from dawn to noon to dusk are the place to start, but later on you'll be able to notice the subtlety of other times. Look for the red shift in light later in the day and then see how you feel under twilight or moonlight. These things dramatically affect our mood and mental spaciousness. The challenge is to get outside to experience this. Today is your day to do so.

This evening go into your yard or a nearby area where you can be around twilight. Shut down whatever lights you can or go somewhere that's not as bright. Slow down and hang out in the transition you're witnessing from light to dark. See what it does to your mind. See what it does to the velocity of your thoughts. It may take 30 minutes to see this through, so take your time. We don't go from light to dark by hitting a switch in nature. The subtlety and beauty lie in the transition.

DAY 64

regular breaks daily

Today we'll practice taking little microbreaks. Set a timer on your phone or your desktop to go off every 25 minutes for a 5-minute break. Time your day to expect this, and make sure you take the breaks as they come.

At first you may feel reluctant, because, as usual, you've got *so much stuff to do*. That's fine. Trust me on this one. Taking a 5-minute break every 25 minutes means two breaks per hour.

Okay, now what?

Get up and stretch out for a minute. Stretch into whatever body part calls you to it. Feel for where you're stuck and let that part decompress. The way you do this is simple. Breathe into the afflicted body part as you stretch into it. Allow your consciousness to relax into that body part as the breath fills the area.

Then think about what you need and do some quick exercise. Maybe some squats, lunges, pushups, jumping jacks, or a few downward dogs. Spend 2 to 3 minutes doing something active that gets your blood moving, maybe stretch for a few more seconds, and then go refill your water, run to the restroom, or whatever else you need.

Stay in the habit of keeping the break to only 5 minutes so you don't get carried away. In an 8-hour workday, you'll get 16 of these, so if you missed something, you're only 25 minutes away from being able to get to it.

What does this do for you?

Lots of good things.

First of all, it keeps your blood flowing so you don't fade. This keeps oxygen pumping to the brain and also drives the muscles to metabolize sugars. With your active metabolic rate up, your resting rate stays up as well. This means more calories burned during the day, even while sitting.

It helps keep you focused, clear, and awake—often better than coffee.

An important added benefit is the boost you get in posture. Long, hard hours of sitting make us crunchy. Our shoulders tend to collapse forward, our hip flexors tighten up, and our low backs get cranky. Getting up and working against this tendency helps offset the negative impacts of stagnation from sitting.

Set your timers and keep to this today.

Worst-case scenario: You don't see any benefit (not possible), and you go back to your old habits tomorrow. However, if and when you do see the boost in energy and mood, you'll start to make this a major part of your daily routine and never look back.

Invest some time in yourself, and the time you "lose" will easily be made up in enhanced productivity, more energy, and a fit and limber body you can readily use after a long day.

DAY 65

shower time

D o you savor your shower time? Why? Usually because it's the most privacy you'll get all day. Maybe the hot water helps melt your tense shoulder muscles. Yes, it is therapeutic and nice to get away, but here's the challenge: Unless you have a shower filter that pulls the chlorine out of that water, you're absorbing it through your skin and breathing it through your lungs. This messes with your good bacteria and has a negative influence on your thyroid.

Even if you do filter it, long, hot showers may feel great but they're not good for the environment. Fresh water is a precious resource that we're having challenges with globally. You're likely burning carbon to heat your shower experience. Wars are fought for that fuel.

So how can you get some privacy, relax your body, clean up, and feel like you're ready for your day?

Long showers often come from a *personal-time deficit*. This means you haven't fed the self-care meter, so you lag in the shower and take more time than you should. Today take a look at where you could nudge some more self-love into your life so you're not feeling like you are owed something. Where else can you get it? A morning stretch? Maybe a weekly massage? You'll have to determine what you need and where you can get that. The point of today's exercise is to bring awareness to something that's been running on autopilot.

We tend to shower every day, so it becomes rote, unconscious. We get in there and do the shower thing, but our mind is often elsewhere. We are thinking about the crazy experiences that are still on our mind, and we're standing around wasting water and burning money. It's fine to shower, *but do so consciously*. Maybe focus on your body and pay special attention to each part as you're washing it—that becomes a conscious ritual.

Baths are great if you need some downtime. You can run the bath, drop in some salts and oils, light some candles, and get prepped for some you time. This way you can take a quick shower to rinse off the outside world and then melt into your bath and give it the time you'd like. Stay as long as you'd like and savor the experience. When finished, you can then get a quick rinse and be done with it.

If you were to take a couple of long baths per week, how would that affect the amount of time you stand around in the shower? The real question is, what do you *actually need* to feel whole? It isn't the shower that's giving it to you. The shower is the excuse. Where can you find and *allocate* the time you'd like to feel whole? Find it. Take it and savor it. You'll find that this will affect the time lag you apply to many other activities throughout your day in a profound way.

DAY 66

the rings of a tree

When you look at the rings of a tree, there's a lot of information to decode. You can see a visual imprint of the years past as you note the differences in the seasons. You can see when there was hardship, challenge, and lack of water, and you can also see the good times. Peering back into history, the rings of a tree give us an interesting almanac that references the history of the fallen life form in front of us.

Think about your time on earth in this context today. If you had concentric rings that demarcated the years you've lived, what would they look like? Think of the rough times you've had. What mark did they leave? Did you have some stressful years that took a toll on you? How about some health challenges you had to struggle through? We've all run different miles, but the impact is noted somewhere in our cells, an almanac much like the rings on a tree.

Look into the mirror and study the lines that may be there. Did they come from happy or sad times? Have you had long exposures to the elements, or are you not getting out as much as you'd like? Do you have any scars or replaced parts that you've picked up along the way?

Let's take an accounting of our lives today and journal the years that impacted us the most. Run down the timeline and write the years or eras that had significance. You can go from present day backward and then start from birth and forward again. This way you can recall more items and layer the nuances in. Keep it to the big stuff, the dings and dents you'd see in the rings of a 100-year-old tree.

Now let's think about how you're living your life presently. Are you on a collision course for another nasty notch? Are you in good times or challenging ones?

This exercise helps us gain some perspective on the big picture of life. We are all tall trees that eventually fall. What will be written on our biological record when we do? The bigger exercise is to then draw from some past lessons and navigate life with a bit more finesse. The big hits take a lot out of us. Weathering too many harsh winters may temper us, but it can also draw on our life force too rapidly.

How can you adjust your growth to balance out some of these trends? What's your vision for the long haul, and have you planned for those years? The anxiety comes from not feeling secure about the future. Today think about what you could do to find some peace there. Can you reallocate some funds toward a rainy day investment? Can you change a lifestyle habit that won't serve you in the long run? Take a look at where you may be challenged on your future trajectory, and make some micro adjustments today.

Looking back at your life many years from now, would you determine that the struggle you're currently wrestling with was worth it? It is your call to make.

DAY 67

building a legacy

D o you ever think about your legacy? Well, today you're going to! If you only have a limited time left on this planet, you're like the rest of us. Whether you're juicing kale, taking ice baths, avoiding processed everything, or snorting ginseng, you're still eventually going to exit this place. What will your lasting legacy be?

Most people shift the attention of this onto their kids. They feel they've brought up some nice children and they can pull over and consider parenting a solid handoff. That's nice that you've run those miles, but what else have you done? What impact have you personally made to change your corner of the world? Today we lean into the work that remains to be done in your life.

What cause is the most important to you? What injustice can you not bear to witness? What do you see around you that keeps you up at night?

It is time to throw your hat in the ring.

The world has many problems, and they keep multiplying because too many people sit on the sidelines and assume the challenges are too big or that someone else is going to handle them.

There is nobody else.

Those people are either watching TV or have their own passions to pursue. If something sparks interest or frustration in you, that's a good clue that it is your burden to resolve. It is your karmic work.

What would you like written on your tombstone? Are you happy with the current story of your life, or is it lacking a little in substance? If you knew you were going to die anyway, then what could you boldly commit your life to that would make a real difference? What words can you visualize on that tombstone that would make you happy and proud? Now start writing those words. Not tomorrow, today. Whether you're well on your way to some amazing legacy or you still lack clarity on what to do, today is the day to do something important toward that goal. Take a step, even a tiny one that will move the world ever so slightly in the direction of some good you'd like to see here.

Perhaps you were thinking you'll get to that when you're finished working and can retire. Nope. You'll have less energy, more pain, less motivation, and no trees to look at by then. Do something today.

Start now. Look deeply into the legacy you'd like to leave for the world and start drawing up a plan to make that a reality, today. Then do one small thing that feels like it is moving you in that direction. You may only have a few hours per week to devote to legacy projects for now, but that's okay. You need to spark some life energy with some movement, and then it'll take on a life of its own. Waiting to start living is the greatest sin. The longer you wait, the more excuses you'll have to *keep waiting*. Then what? Then you die a normal death with no lasting imprint on the world? Not you.

Today you take a look at where you want that legacy to end up and then start making a plan to earn the words on that tombstone. Calculate how many years you think you have left and see what it'll take to make the impression you want. It may be a huge lift and require people to help you. That's fine. People follow leaders with clear vision, enthusiasm, and the spark of life in their eyes. Where is yours?

Find it. Spark it.

DAY 68

time in bed

The bed is for sleep and making love. That should be it, but too often we use that space for multitasking, like everything else in our lives. So today you're going to take everything else you do there and move it to another place. It is a sacred space where your mind knows it is time to close the mental windows and shut down for the night. Some light reading is okay, but there's certainly no sanity in doing bills in bed. If you're staring at a screen, you're putting yourself in a compromised state for optimal sleep.

Today let's look at your sleep-hygiene habits. Are you properly decelerating in the evening and getting ready for sleep? Are you keeping the craziness of the outside world out of your bedroom? Nighttime should typically be *slow time*.

Have a look around your bedchamber today. Is the room messy? If so that'll reflect back on your brain. Before going to sleep tonight, clear out your space. Do you have a TV in there? It is time to shut that down permanently. All the best sleep experts agree that the TV is incredibly disruptive to your sleep. It also kills intimacy and boots up senseless noise in your brain when you should be clearing the deck.

How cool do you keep it in there? The optimal temperature (this varies for people) has been found to be around 68°F. A cooler room helps you sleep. Walk through and pull out any unnecessary electronics. Who knows what all of those buzzing contraptions are doing to us? We're so sedated and vulnerable when we sleep. Let's not bake in harmful waves of edgy energy.

Now think about safety. How safe do you feel at night? Are there loud sounds that jolt you up? Is there a remedy for the snoring beast who sleeps next to you? Maybe you need a deadbolt on the doors if you're in a high-crime area. Maybe a dog would help (or maybe your dog is the snorer and needs to get used to sleeping in the living room). The point is to make your home feel safe so you can surrender to sleep. Sleep is about letting go and falling into the still darkness of the night.

It sounds obvious that darkness is the opposite of light, but take a look around your bedroom today and hunt for all the items that emit light, even a little bit. This is light pollution, and it will subtly impact your sleep. Get rid of it.

The next step is to think about all the activities you bring to the bed. Are you making calls? Are you idling on social media? What are you doing in bed other than sleeping and making love? Make a list and start to come up with a plan to eradicate all of these items. You're free to do them in life but *not in bed*. If you hold this line, something magical happens. Nighttime gets more peaceful, and your rest and recovery cycles improve. Time slows down at night. That leads to a better mood, more energy, and more spaciousness in your consciousness. You have more time to think and take care of yourself, and you will get more done each day.

It's usually the little things that make a big difference over time in our lives. Today take back your bedroom and make it a safe haven for deep sleep and better intimacy. Try it for a few nights in a row and you'll notice a profound difference.

DAY 69

how many heartbeats
do I have left?

Your heart beats about 100,000 times in one day. That's about 35 million times in a year and about 2.5 billion times in an average lifetime. That's it. That's all you get.

If you had lots of money—say $2.5 billion—you'd feel rich. Now, that being said, the average worldwide human lifespan is 71 years. So if you're 46 years old, you've already burned through $1.6 billion in life cash. That leaves $900 million to go. That's still a lot, but at what point do you start to get worried? Well, regardless of your current age, that answer should be "right now," if you're not living the life you want.

Let's look at how you're rolling through life and see if your current trajectory is making those heartbeats count toward your overall satisfaction and happiness or not. If you're stuck in a holding pattern and don't see a way out for another 6 years, that's 210 million heartbeats in the wrong direction—almost 10 percent of your net time worth. Does that make sense, or do you need to make some adjustments right now?

Look at your personal heartbeat math today. Which ones were the most memorable? How many days have passed uneventfully or consumed by worries or distractions that don't feel worth the currency? They were probably fine, but then how many were beating during bad times? How many under extreme stress and duress? How many happy heartbeats would you need to invest to counter those days or years?

There's no hard and true answer here, just a shift in perspective. It's a good practice to think about this concept from time to time, in case life has gotten us distracted. We can often find ourselves pulled over in the highway of life, simply idling somewhere we'd rather not be. Are you there now? If so, then how do you make a plan to change direction?

The key is to understand that your time here is a gift and when those beats have passed, your time is up. What else would you like to do and experience on this planet? What places do you need to see? If you'd like to hike a famous mountain, what shape do you need to be in to do so? Some things can't wait till retirement. Think this through today, and start to make a plan to support your dreams and aspirations along your trajectory.

You still have plenty of heartbeats left to experience some real joy and happiness in the world. For the next few days, think about making sure that something happens every day that allows you to feel that.

DAY 70

bath time

Today's item will probably have to wait till this evening. Find at least 30 to 60 minutes of uninterrupted time to take a nice, long bath. It may have to be when the kids go to bed or maybe while they're in school. You don't simply *find* time for things like this: You have to *make time.*

Elbow and shoulder out an hour (ideally) for a nice, long bath. You'll need a couple of things that can be found in any drugstore.

1. Epsom salts
2. Some lavender essential oil (or frankincense); there are lots of blends that are relaxing. Aromatherapy is great.
3. A candle
4. Calming music

Take a quick shower before running the bathwater. Add 1 to 2 cups of Epsom salts and let the tub fill. Add the essential oil before you get in. Light a candle (or a few) and play your music. Turn off all the other lights. If you're playing music off of your phone, make sure you put it in airplane mode. This is your time! Set an alarm if you have limited time and can't lose track. This way you can relax into the space you've created.

Get in slowly and get comfortable.

The next step is to start breathing to your lower abdomen; the vibe is low and slow. Take at least 20 deep breaths and then stop to check in and see how you feel. If you sense any discomfort, relax into it; let it melt into the tub.

Once you feel at ease again, go back to your lower-belly breathing. Keep going through cycles of this and see how much more relaxed you can get. Occasionally, stuff comes up that you can simply observe and let pass, like layers of an onion. Let them peel away. Visualize the tub absorbing all of your toxins as the magnesium (which comes naturally in Epsom salts) absorbs into your skin. Magnesium helps boost the activity of your mitochondria, which helps energize you. It also calms your nerves and helps you sleep.

When ready, drain the tub and slowly get up. Run the shower again, but this time make sure the temperature is slightly lower than normal body temperature. It doesn't need to be freezing, just cool enough to seal all of your energy centers and invigorate your *qi* (energy).

Taking time for yourself may seem indulgent, but watch how you feel in the week after rewarding yourself with such a concentrated amount of self-love. You'll find that the investment of some quality time goes a long way.

Most of us go through our weeks complaining of fatigue and no personal time. When we let it stretch out too long, we long for far-off lands, megacleanses, and career changes. Maybe a little bit of regular TLC is all we need to stay balanced. We feel time prosperity when we press pause and *take the time* for ourselves. You'll find that your tank is filled and you can be a better you all week.

DAY 71

cardio time

"Fast" in our culture is tied to mental speed. We handle multiple balls in the air, crunch deadlines, skip meals. That's stupid fast. The velocity that actually brings up the heart rate in a healthy way is a whole other beast. This gets our physiology humming. It pumps our endorphins, pushes toxins out via our lymphatic system, and effectively boosts mitochondria and energy output. It's the good stuff.

So today's lesson is to play with your heart rate and sense the shift in the quality of time. Go to a park or the gym or find some space at home and get prepared to jam. Stretch out and warm up your body so you don't hurt yourself.

Cardio workouts are good for your heart and overall well-being: no newsflash there. Today let's look at cardio under a different lens. This will provide a slightly different perspective that can prove useful in your daily life.

When we elevate our heart rate, it is like a clock that starts to tick faster. The blood is being driven through the vessels by ionic gradients, and the heart is helping push and direct the flow of it within the body. The velocity goes up, which delivers more energy, oxygen, and nutrients to the brain and the muscles more effectively.

Time may be moving along at the same click outside of your body, but it has certainly sped up on the inside. *This gives us range.* It becomes much easier to understand how to find slow when you have a grasp on fast.

When ready, start to run, bike, row, and swim. Get warmed up for about 10 minutes and then cut loose and go to your maximum intensity. Let your heart rate get way up there, and stay at your max for about 1 to 2 minutes (depending on your health history and fitness level). For most people this is at around 160 to 180 beats per minute. You can do a test at your local gym to find what's called your maximum VO_2. Or you can calculate your maximum heart rate by subtracting your age from 220. It is helpful to know, but it's essentially when your chest is pounding and it becomes harder to catch your breath.

Then slow it way down and let your heart rate recover to around 110 beats per minute. This may take a few minutes depending on the kind of shape you're in, so pay attention to how your body feels.

When back to 110, turn up the speed and get back to your max and stay there for another couple of minutes. Again, come back down and recover. Do this two to five times and then go stretch out. Slow it way down and catch your breath. See how you feel.

This exercise is wonderful for showing us the range in our perception of the quality of time. It speeds up and slows down in relation to our own physiology. There's a powerful lesson in this. First off, it teaches that having superior cardio fitness gives us more dynamic range both physically and psychologically. Second, it shows that our consciousness can shift with our burn rate and that a quick phase shift in physiology can profoundly impact our perception of reality. It'll teach you a lot about yourself and also give you much more control over how you run the ship you call life. Enjoy the burn.

DAY 72

time in the dark

Today's activity will actually have to wait till this evening, when it starts getting dark. Quality time in low light is how our ancestors lived for generations. When the sun went down, they'd wind down by candlelight or sit around a fire and hang out.

We were accustomed to the darkness, and it was both soothing to the mind and therapeutic for the body. How? The darkness signals our brains to start shutting down and preparing for sleep. This is when our body temperature drops so we can go into maintenance mode and repair tissue, grow, process our hectic day, and, frankly, hit reset. We need the darkness to help trigger this.

Tonight take a few minutes to slow down in the dark. If your family is around, maybe find a room to hang out in, or, better yet, get them involved. Turn off the lights and simply sit for a moment.

Start breathing to your lower abdomen and keep your eyes closed for the first minute or two. When you've gathered yourself, it is time to open your eyes. Look into and through the darkness. Let your eyes adjust. What subtle light do you see? Maybe the glow of a clock, some electronics, or some device on the wall? Maybe there's light coming in from the street outside or under the door from the hallway outside. Is it possible to see moonlight?

Breathe slowly and deeply to your lower abdomen and simply take note of the subtle hues of light in your dark room. Does it freak you out or make you uncomfortable? Why? You're in your own house, and it was safe a minute ago. Why is the absence of artificial light making the same room scary? Breathe into this. Relax into your body.

So many of us are petrified of the dark for no logical reason. You're not running around, so you needn't worry about injury. You can use your phone's light to get up and walk to the light switch when we're finished. It's okay—just sit and hang. Relax into the darkness of the room.

Over time, you'll notice how soothing it is to be in the *absence of light*. This is what it is supposed to be like at night, what we're biologically accustomed to. When we spend a few minutes in the darkness, our brains get the message and start signaling the body to *slow down* and decelerate into the night. This has a profound effect on our perception of time.

Consider turning this into a nightly ritual rather than a onetime activity, and see how it changes your evening routine and ability to get to sleep. Imagine how peaceful it would be if you ended your day reconnecting with the natural rhythms of light, not the television blaring at you while you fall asleep or even the glow of your device while you read in bed. The darkness will help turn your energy dial down. Get comfortable with it and breathe deeply into this space. It may be hard at first, but with some quality time spent, you'll be able to use darkness to slow time and relax your body and mind quite effectively.

DAY 73

enlisting help

Are you time deprived because you have too much to do? Do you feel like you don't have any help and all of your hours get sucked into keeping the mechanisms of your life going, whether it's the whole family, the whole office, the whole social group, or some combination of all of the above? Well, you're not alone. It doesn't have to be that way though.

Enlisting help is not easy, because we're all control freaks in some way. "I need it done *this way* and in *this order*." It can feel like our job is to be the one greasing the wheels behind the scenes, and we may even not be sure what we'd do if we weren't always busy dealing with the logistics.

But not being able to get help is exhausting, and not asking for help will lead to burnout. Today let's do something about it.

Look back at yesterday (or a better example of an average day) and start writing down what you did from waking until you went to bed. Try to pick apart every little detail of the day, from bathroom time to errands. This may take a few minutes but is a worthwhile pursuit. Jot down each activity on its own line and keep firing down the list. If you skip a step, put it in when you remember it and keep going. Write the approximate time it took to do each task to the right of it.

Once you have your list (and, yes, it's never complete because you do a million things daily), start going down and reading each item. Put a little star next to each item that you think you can get someone to help you with. Depending on your finances, this can range from "watching the kids" or "getting groceries" to "doing my taxes," "cooking dinner," or "checking the movie time." Fly down the list and take note of the items where someone could technically help you out. Even if you think you can't afford the help, put the star for now to indicate which tasks don't *have* to be completed by you.

Next do another pass where you put another star on items you've already marked for items that you feel you can enlist help without significant strain. Maybe a friend or family member can help or you can start a carpool with neighbors. Maybe you don't have to cook something new every single night and can try batch cooking twice per week. Maybe someone else can be the activities planner once in a while. These become the first items to start considering.

Here's the deal. Today you can order most things online at a reasonable rate. That means far fewer trips to the store. Think about all the driving, parking, and fuss you avoid. Boom: There's some time reabsorbed. What about a helper? You can get a virtual assistant online (try www.upwork.com or www.brickworkindia.com) for as low as $3 per hour. Are there tasks you can hand off and gladly pay $3 per hour to do? If so, you'll be making a nice family in some village happy.

Do you need help at work? Maybe you need another critical hire or some interns. Think about it. The 80/20 rule (the Pareto principle) states that 80 percent of your revenue comes from 20 percent of your activity, so what's the 20 percent that's actually moving you forward? Where are you wasting time, and where can you enlist help?

If you are swamped in your domestic life, look at the same principle. Where does your time need to go, and where is it going? What can you cut out, and where can you get help? There are billions of people on this planet, and plenty are fine at the menial tasks you shouldn't be doing. Reabsorb this time and let people help you. Today choose one item on your starred list and make a plan for delegating it. Commit to letting someone else help you execute this task, then take it off your list and don't let it back on. If your first idea for how to delegate doesn't work, find another way to get it done that doesn't involve you.

DAY 74

time on a lake

Have you ever wondered why lakes are so peaceful? One reason is because they represent stopped time. Think about it. Water comes down and flows through the soil and into a creek or a river. It moves and represents the passing of time. You're never looking at the same stream. A lake, on the other hand, is where this flow stops (or at least stalls). The water accumulates and sits. It feeds plants on the edges, fish, bugs, algae, and much more. There's a serenity to it that captivates us: It slows us down.

Water likes a resting place, and so do we. Today look to find a few minutes to stop the flow of your day. Find a lake or a pond and sit by it; if you don't know where a body of water is, look at a map of your local area. You will probably be surprised to find one closer to you than you think! It doesn't have to be huge. Make time to get there for this exercise.

Contemplate the nature of the beauty in front of you. Take several deep breaths down to your lower abdomen and settle into your body. Think about the flow of your day like a rushing stream. See the events since the morning and see the water tumbling along your timeline. Come to the present moment and visualize a beautiful lake where you've now stopped the flow of the day and are taking some time to reflect. The lake is deeper than the stream. The water is still, and it is quiet. See the difference and bring your thoughts to align with the metaphor. Slow your flow and "sit" in your lake. Hang here for several minutes and allow the change in velocity to settle in. It is the same water you're accustomed to, but the quality of time has changed. It is now your turn to change with it.

Slow your breath and enjoy the serenity of your lake. When thoughts of the rest of your day come up, simply move your gaze to the other end of the lake, where there's an outlet for the water. You can see the water start to pick up in velocity and become a creek again. That's fine—you'll go there soon enough. You know that speed. Smile and bring yourself back to the comfort and stillness of the middle of your lake.

Hang here as long as you can. If you can't get to a real lake, visualize the sights and sounds. If you are fortunate enough to have access to one, well, enjoy a little longer.

Stay here and feel the slowed flow. This water is a perfect reflection of your relationship with time. It can slow and it can quicken. Right now you're in a peaceful lake. Maybe downstream you'll be rafting some crazy white water, but remember, that experience is also drawing from the same water you're sitting in now.

When we understand how water changes phases, we can enjoy each one. They all have a flavor and a vibe. Time is the same.

When you're ready to flow back into your day, move your awareness to the outlet of your lake and see yourself flowing down a stream again. Not too fast: Enjoy the ride and ease back into it.

DAY 75

bird-watching

Have you ever stopped to watch the birds? When is the last time you noticed them—watched, listened, or followed?

There's an incredible language of life all around us, and it is being sung by the birds. In the wild, our ancestors were acutely aware of the birdsong. It would let them know if a predator was coming, or if there was rain, trouble, food, or frankly, any other news. They are communicating about critical events in the natural world, and all we need to do is learn to listen. There are alarm calls, love songs, and much more.

Today your practice is to spend a few minutes tapping into this amazing realm.

Step outside and find a comfortable place to simply listen. Take a few breaths to your lower abdomen and center yourself. Tune your ear to all the sounds around you. Take a minute to settle into this. You'll likely hear human sounds, machines, and plenty more. That's fine.

Tune your ears to the sounds of the birds. Listen to those and slowly tune out the other sounds. If you're lucky enough to live closer to nature, this will be that much easier.

Keep your breath slow and low, and relax into your body. Listen. Tune out all else and find the bird sounds. There's no need to watch them at first—just follow the sounds.

How many do you notice? How many different ones? Are they happy or stressed, distant or nearby?

There's no game to win here, just another world to visit. Keep your breathing slow and simply hang with your winged friends for a few minutes.

You're welcome to watch them play in the future, but this practice is primarily focused on the *sounds* first. Get acquainted with the birdsong and tune into their chirps and songs today. Once you're connected to it, you can always go back to this magical place. The more time you spend here, the more your ear gets tuned and greater subtlety emerges. It's an amazing language, filled with nuances we tend to ignore. If you love it, download an app that'll teach you the bird calls in your area.

The birds are pure. They come from the beauty of nature and, unlike many other wild animals, still live among us in our daily lives. They can serve as an easy anchor *back to our natural state* once we learn to tune into their world.

Listen and enjoy.

DAY 76

car time

Today we take our time back from traffic.

The average American spends an average of an hour per day in the car. That's time crunching your spine, tightening your hips, collapsing your posture, and slowing down your metabolism. Not using car time efficiently is a form of slow suicide, and today you're going to do something about this.

Taking your time back revolves around finding the places where time is dead and wasted and reabsorbing them into something that serves you.

The simple hack you are probably already doing is to make your phone calls. It's great to be able to catch up with friends and family to make a commute easier to bear. Some people probably make a lot of work calls; that can certainly be an efficient use of time, although I'd argue that it won't do anything to help reduce your stress. But how much talk time is necessary versus simply filling the air and wasting your breath?

Only you can answer that.

Are there books you've been meaning to read? Audiobooks are amazing in the car. Imagine how much you'd benefit if you used your commuting hours to get smarter, learn something, be entertained, or at least feel caught up. There are podcasts to listen to, university lectures to absorb, and languages to learn. If any of this sits in your long-term goals, then download, rent, or buy something today for your next commute.

Say you're wiped out and need to catch your breath though. Okay. Then car time becomes about calming music and a serene space you create. The phone then becomes a distraction and robs you of this precious quiet time to decompress. If you need it, *take it*. That often means hitting "ignore" on the ringing phone.

Another key piece to optimizing car time is keeping your body engaged and your postural muscles active even while sitting there. This means using the left foot to push against the footrest so your pelvis is even and both legs are working. It also means pulling your lower traps together and aligning your neck so you're not slouching the whole way. These are the muscles you engage by having your hands up to your sides with the elbows down and drawing the elbows in toward your back pockets. It looks like you're making a "W" as you bring the elbows in and then relax them. Pull in your abdominals and engage your core even when sitting there. If you really want to be a champ, pull your pubic area up from the pubococcygeus (PC) muscle several times per minute. That's called a Kegel exercise, and it will build your pelvic floor, strengthen your core, and improve your sex life. Now we're talking.

The moral of the story is, don't let car time be dead time. It is *your time*. Treat it with respect and use it for what you need. It may be different from day to day, and that's fine. It is your time, and you need to determine where it's best spent each day.

So what do you need to balance yourself today? How best can you optimize the use of your time in order to feel more whole? Traffic may be a harsh reality for many of us, but we don't need to collapse and surrender.

DAY 77

time and weight gain

S o many people are concerned with weight gain today that it has become an enormous industry. Let's look at it through the lens of time today and see if we can liberate some power.

Fat is essentially stored energy in our bodies. When our caloric input is greater than that which we exert, the body converts the excess energy into fat and stores it away for a crisis situation. In the old days, food was scarce and we never knew when the next meal would come. Today this isn't the case.

Beyond the calories-in/out model of weight gain, we now know that the body also uses fat to help protect us against environmental toxins. We will pack on fat around our organs to help defend them against chemical invaders, and this visceral fat is unhealthy. It messes with our blood sugar levels, our metabolic rate, and our self-image.

So let's unpack this today. Fat is stored energy we have yet to expend, and it is being used to shield us from the toxins around us. We can use this knowledge to our advantage.

The energy we consumed yesterday didn't have an outlet via activity. Let's start there. This means that more activity today with fewer calories would shift that math and allow us to dip into our energy savings. This is the traditional model for weight loss. We now know that it's more complicated than this, but it certainly still applies. The important thing to remember here is getting more active and consuming fewer calories in the form of empty carbs (if you're overweight).

Today's gong is a long walk. Take an hour and go at a nice, brisk pace. Go for longer if you can. The key is to get moving and rev up your metabolism. The longer periods of consistent exertion can turn on the fat-burning mode your body would love to be in. If you can do this in nature, even better.

The point is to look at your current weight and determine how much of yesterday you're carrying around today. How can you adjust your burn rate to bring it into balance? If you are carrying extra pounds from yesterday, today is the day to release them so your body can catch up in time. How do you do that? You get the engine revving and turn up the metabolic dial.

DAY 78

time with a tree

Today you need to find a tree. Look around and find one you'd like to hang with. If you're in the desert, find a cactus. If you're on the moon, how the hell did you get this book? Find a tree that you vibe with, and let's hang with it.

Trees are majestic. Their roots dig deep into the ground, and that's where the magic of life happens. Namely, this is where bacteria, Protozoa, viruses, and a host of other life forms work together in the soil at the root nodules of plants to break down inorganic matter and make life possible for YOU. Yeah. The magic that happens at the root of the tree you're looking at allows it to transform the energy of the sun into sugars we live off. It also allows for the tree to turn carbon dioxide in the atmosphere into the oxygen you are breathing right now.

Hey, thanks.

That's the practice for today. Let's take some time and be grateful for this tree. Close your eyes and breathe deeply to your lower abdomen for a few seconds. Now go walk up to your tree and touch it if you can. If not, just keep your eyes on it while doing this practice.

Next visualize roots coming out the bottom of your feet. On the next exhale, push them down a few feet into the ground. On the next inhale, breathe energy and light up those roots all the way to the top of your head. Feel the tree in front of you. Sync up with it while breathing through your imaginary roots. Do this for a minute or two.

Next visualize your roots mingling and twisting around those of the tree. Get connected.

Now start breathing in unison with the tree. You just got taller and more rooted. Take several breaths connecting up like this and use the tree as your extended life antenna. Relax into it and really feel it.

When you're ready to move on, visualize your roots untangling from that of the tree. Take a couple more breaths through your own roots, pulling energy from the ground. Now slowly detach your hands and/or your gaze from the tree. Thank it and bless it before moving on. Keep your own roots in the ground, and work to stay connected and feel the earth under your feet all day today.

Now that you've experienced tree time, play around with other types of trees and plants. You'll notice they have different energies and vibes. Find an oak, and if you're lucky enough to get to a giant redwood, well, enjoy the ride.

DAY 79

your bucket list

Today we think about the list of experiences you'd like to have before you kick the bucket. Excluding all things (which you can't take with you), let's get into the fun, fulfilling, enriching, or decadent experiences you'd like to have before you check out. It may take some time to truly populate this list, so let's relax into this exercise and dig deep.

Think about the obvious ones that are your go-to answers. Maybe it's having dinner in Paris, seeing Machu Picchu, or going into high orbit. It may be living in Africa for a year or seeing hot air balloons in New Mexico. Think about all the experiences you've wanted to have, and write down the ones that need to be on your list.

As you scan your mind for them, keep listing more and more. Dig back into your past all the way to childhood. What experiences did you crave then? List those, too. You may find that many of your current desires echo ones from your childhood, which remain open loops in your psyche. Go through and keep listing them for a few minutes.

When ready, let's take a look at what kind of time it'll take to do all of this. To the right of each item, put the approximate time you'd need to set aside to have that experience and do it right. It can only be marked as complete if you're satisfied with the experience, so make sure you don't allocate a day for some far-off adventure. Some of the items you'll find can indeed be done in half a day. Take skydiving for instance: For most people that's a day trip, even though it seems so far off in our mind.

Go through and assign times to each item and then study the list for a bit. How much total time would it take to complete all of your items to your satisfaction? It may be months or years. That's fine. Now let's look at your current age and state of health. Make an honest assessment of how many years you think you reasonably have left here on planet Earth. Let's say that number is 20 years.

Now let's look at what you'd need to do in order to get in most if not all of your desired experiences within that time frame. You may want to take the more physically challenging ones on sooner and not leave them till you're too old. You can maybe do something each quarter to work off your list and plan a bigger trip annually. Perhaps you have quite a long list going. That may require a monthly adventure.

This is where reality sets in. You'll need time *and* money to get to many of these. That's fine. If these experiences will enrich your soul and make you happy, then we need to look at where your current time and money are being spent. How can you reallocate these resources to invest in working off your list?

The math may not be simple, but it will force you to think about the important stuff. How can you work balance into your life so that you have passion, adventure, and fulfillment built into what you do? Why not do this?

Think about your current outflow of time, money, and energy and see where you'd need to redirect them in order to have your desired experiences. It'll make you much more conscious of how you spend your time idly. It'll show you how precious it is.

Invest your time into your dreams and you'll live a fulfilled life.

DAY 80

time to heal your body

.

Our bodies need time to unravel and heal. When's the last time you left some space for this? Normally, we bang around, trying to get through our days, and it leaves bumps, bruises, aches, and fatigue. We assume there'll be time to lick our wounds and heal, but when? The answer is when we get sick, which is often too late. Our bodies are amazingly resilient. They take on so much for us, and we seldom stop to honor them or give them some time and space to recover.

Today take a few minutes and connect with your body. Breathe deeply down to your lower abdomen and relax into the moment. Then ask your body what it needs. Stay quiet and listen to what it tells you.

It may alert you to aches in your neck and shoulders. You may become aware of a strain from a recent workout or a pain from an uncomfortable belt or shoe. Maybe what you hear is that you're exhausted and feeling it in your bones. That's common.

So what's it going to take to give your body a little restoration today?

Take 5 to 15 minutes (or more if you can) to dedicate to your body. Do whatever comes to you in response to your query. For example, if your low back is sore and tired, get on the ground and stretch, roll around, ball up, do some yoga, or whatever you intuitively feel will help. This may not be the end-all answer to your back woes, but it is finally a step in the right direction. What direction? An orientation around self-care. From here you can seek out professional help and move toward a solution.

If your neck hurts, roll it out, heat your trapezius muscles, and look at your alignment. The best way to do this is to stand against a wall and see how comfortably your head rests on the wall. If you're off, look at your posture at your desk or in the car.

Knees and ankles need TLC. Ice may be your friend if they are inflamed. Strengthening the surrounding muscles is often the solution for these joints. The key is to research your remedy, go to a professional, and ultimately, do what it takes to mend your body.

Self-care is the missing ingredient in our modern lifestyle. We've erroneously come to believe that we can crush it all day every day and pull into the doctor's office to get fixed up quickly. This is insane, yet we all do it on some level. Not today.

Today is the first day of the rest of your life. Your task is to tap in, ask your body what it needs, and then *give it what it needs*. Getting into the habit of this will help you in life. Learning to stop time and *check in* is a paradigm shift that'll drive future good decisions that will be fruitful.

Your body needs rest. It needs space and recovery time. Today we honor this. See what comes of it.

Good things come to those who love up their bodies. Today that's you.

DAY 81

vow of silence

Today is going to be an interesting day.

The spiritual practice of taking a vow of silence is therapeutic. We spew our energy out on wasted words all day every day, and this practice will help you bring it back. We live in a world of noise, and we've become accustomed to making noise to chime into the insane symphony.

Today we stop that. The gold standard is to take off and avoid everyone, but that may not be practical. A step down is to avoid any unnecessary conversation all day. Tell people around you what you're doing so they don't hit you with "what's wrong?" energy all day. Keep to yourself and only speak when absolutely necessary. If you have work calls, obviously take them, but remain aware of how much you speak. Practice economy of speech all day if you must talk. Think through what you're going to say, and be intentional, clear, and pointed. There's no reason to take the sweetness out of your tone either—don't get weird. Think of the word "hi." How many ways can you say it? Try filling your heart with love and enthusiasm before you say the word. How different does that sound? Notice how much the energy behind a single word can change the vibe and tone of a whole interaction. Less can be more. Eye contact and a smile mean way more than empty words.

Step away and be silent as often as you can today. Save your breath and circulate it deep down in your lower belly. Notice how much of this vital breath you tend to squander in your life. Notice how much you talk for the sake of talking. Why? It's usually a habit from childhood or an anxious way to fill the empty space around you. We're learning how to stop time and enjoy the slower velocity of silence and slowness today. Learn to get comfortable here. If things come up, write them down and think about why. In the silence come the undercurrents of our shadows. We get to see the uncomfortable things that are keeping us saddled and draining our energy.

If you want more time and energy, you must become aware of the parasitic thoughts and emotions that are holding you back. You cannot see them (or hear them in this case) if you insist on spinning out of control day after day.

When you do get a chance to "go full emersion" in this practice, pick a day when you know you won't be bothered and tell your world that you're doing a silent retreat all day. If someone speaks to you, write back on a pad or even on your phone that you're not speaking today. Smile and move off into your space. Ideally, you'll build in some seclusion and personal space to enjoy this process. It helps anchor your mind and slow the chaos. In fact, you'll be startled at first at how loud it is upstairs, but as the hours pass, things will get better and you'll feel the difference.

Enjoy the silence.

DAY 82

trading time

We trade time for things every day. We trade it for money, connection, favors, and future fun (vacation or retirement). We can invest our time now for a vacation later and bank certain hours at our desks for (usually fewer) hours at a beach somewhere nice. This all works out and makes sense in the grand scheme of things as long as we get what we need out of the exchange.

Have you ever gone on a trip where you were planning on relaxing only to get swept up into touristy activities, logistical complications, and obligations from home and wound up having a mediocre time? This happens often. The challenge is when you were counting on this time to catch your breath, slow your roll, and decompress a bit. You put in hundreds of hours of hectic work time to buy the time on that escape, and, frankly, the experience didn't deliver. That sucks.

We can be dismissive about these occurrences at the time but need to think about what happens to our life over the next few months upon return. We come back with less energy, enthusiasm, and drive from trips like this. What we needed was a healthy reset, and we came back wanting. We then have less patience and energy going to work each day, and the next vacation isn't for a while. This leads to depression, foul moods, and lots more coffee consumption.

Let's think about this today. Are you getting enough value from your time trades? Is the exchange fair and equitable, or are you losing out on what you need? This is personal math that needs to work for you and your individual needs. Think about the time you take for yourself and the exchange that goes into getting it. Does the value stack up for you?

GOOD MATH:

Time In < Value Out

BAD MATH:

Time In > Value Out

The exchange gets interesting when you bring up the quality and value of the daily time you spend in your life so that it doesn't have such an expensive and heavy burden. That way, there's less time debt to pay off on your breaks. Eventually, you take some nice breaks and get out of a bad time deficit, and life takes on a new flavor: It starts to be fun again.

This is where renewed enthusiasm comes from.

Look at how you trade your time today and make whatever adjustments are necessary to maximize the value you get from the time put in.

DAY 83

time under the moon

When's the last time you stopped to check out the moon? What phase was it in? Do you remember how it made you feel? Usually, when we give ourselves a chance to look up at night, we have a profound moment. Maybe we reflect on where we've been, stop to give thanks, or even simply exhale and take in the magnificence of the moon.

The moon is a rock floating about 250,000 miles away from us, and yet we can see it clearly with the naked eye. *Think about that.* Take a second to absorb the size and the scale of this thing that's dangling up there, patiently waiting for you to stop and look up so it can smile back down on you.

The moon has been given a feminine quality by the ancients, much like the earth. Stars emit light. Solid planets and moons reflect it. So what you're looking upon is sunlight bouncing off the surface of a huge rock in the sky. This rock affects tides, moods, and thoughts in people. It pulls on us.

For thousands of years, our ancestors tracked time and the seasons with the moon. Women tended to menstruate with it, and men hunted by moonlight at night. It played a central part in our culture and influenced the timing of our events. Today we forget to look up. We may see it on occasion but usually don't take the time to savor it. This is folly.

Tonight's gong item is to go find the moon and spend at least 10 minutes with it. When is moonrise and moonset? If it's a new moon, find out where it's supposed to be. Is it waxing or waning? Is it full? Look at the glistening moonlight on the objects (preferably natural ones) around you. See them in this new light, and stop to *reflect on their reflection*. The moon is reflecting the sun so brightly that it's shining that light down on us; we are twice or thrice removed from the original sunrays. How does this distillation make things look? Does it bring out other qualities in the objects you're looking at?

Take some time and learn to see by moonlight. Things have a softer and more calming quality under the moon. Time slows down, and so do we. Our ancestors didn't have to learn this, because they lived it and basked in it. We need to put in some effort to find it again. The good news is that tonight's your first night back on the right side of this equation. Tonight you get to rekindle an age-old relationship with a loving friend who's been patiently waiting for you.

DAY 84

learning animal tracks

Our ancestors used to glean volumes of information from the tracks of animals. They'd know if an animal was pregnant, hurt, in a hurry, or even being playful. Obviously, reading tracks of other humans was also a relevant skill we possessed. When out in the wild, the tracks of birds, mammals, insects, and reptiles give us a powerful story about the happenings in that area. The tracks are often documented in the soil (or substrate) and show the effects of weather, wind, or sun. We can know approximately when an animal passed through a given area based on its tracks and what direction it was headed in.

In short, there are volumes of information trapped in nature that document the passing of time all around us. Today's practice is to anchor in on this and simply take note of the tracks you see. If you look hard enough, you'll find them. It may be off to the side of the road, or you may need to go to a park if you're in an urban jungle.

They are there. When's the last time you took notice of them?

That's your practice today. It's about getting out of your comfort zone and learning to observe your environment. Find some tracks and see what you make of them. Guess what they could be and then do something our ancestors never had access to (but didn't need). Look them up. Chances are you have a smartphone on you, so take a guess and look up the image of the tracks of the animal's print you think you're looking at. Were you right? If not, look up the common animals in your area and look for their tracks. Which one is it? Even pigeons make tracks, so all you need to do is slow down and observe.

This may be totally new to you. That's good. It'll help anchor you into something real that's been under your nose all of these years. Know that this information was critical at one point not too long ago. Walking out into the woods could be dangerous, and fresh wolf tracks would mean something serious if you saw them. Where's that in your life now? Maybe the distant sound of a siren that doesn't pertain to you? The threat of death brings us to life. Death is real.

The point is to anchor into something real and learn about it today. Situational awareness used to keep us alive. Now we've shut it down and are less present because of this.

What you're doing with this exercise is looking back in time. Something happened, and you're seeing the reflection of this event on the earth. It may be the simple daily meanderings of a squirrel, but stop and savor the beauty of that for a moment. We're all so self-absorbed that the plants and animals around us are taken for granted. No wonder we have global warming. If all of us were to appreciate the life surrounding us, we'd be less likely to blindly look away when the trucks take all of our trash to the dump.

Slow down and find some tracks today. Learn what they are and spend a few minutes enjoying a new skill set. You may find that other tracks keep popping up for you in the ensuing weeks as you've opened your awareness to this new world. That's good. This information unlocks genetic memory in you—the *sane* genes that remember what it's like to enjoy life's simple pleasures.

DAY 85

times with low sleep

Whether it was in the early days of parenting, cranking through grad school, or some other time in your life, you've probably had periods when you knew about low sleep all too well. Sometimes life comes at you fast and there's less time to build recovery into your schedule. But sleeplessness makes us tired, weary, moody, less enthusiastic, and unfocused. If you stay in this state for too long, you probably know well that you'll start to see negative effects on your career, relationships, health, or mood—possibly all of the above. For most people, low sleep is anything less than 7 or 8 hours.

There are lots of ways to get through tough times. Think about the last time you went through a spurt of sleeplessness (you might be in the midst of it now). How did you handle it? Did you drink lots of caffeine? Did you take pills? Did you work out more to compensate for it? Think back about that time and recall where you went mentally. Now consider what changed to bring about the low-sleep period. Maybe you had good rituals that you stopped protecting vigilantly? Maybe it was a major life change, such as a baby or a move to a new and noisy environment? Did it have something to do with your stress level, either at work or in a relationship?

When we're in compressed time like that, it can feel like there's no end in sight. The sleeplessness makes us feel crazy. We start to lose hope as our energy starts to wane and our light begins to flicker.

Where did you have to go mentally to get through the tough times? Did you wish time would speed up or slow down?

Today's practice is about gaining some clarity and perspective on the mental state you were in last time you were sleepless and sleep poor. When you were low on sleep and ready to explode, how did it shift your relationship with time? Did you lose track of it? Were you frustrated enough to forget to smell the roses? Chances are you were. We all go through those times.

The real lesson comes now though. In reflecting back to those difficult days, what would you do differently, knowing what you now know? What better ways can you cope in the future? The current version of you has more wisdom and the benefit of hindsight. Examine that era in your life and look at what could be deemed mistakes. Did you cut some corners that ended up costing you more time and grief? Did you hurt the people closest to you? You may not be able to take some things back, but you certainly can plan for better sleep hygiene in the future. How can you build more sleep and recovery into your schedule?

Time compression can bring out the worst in us. Looking back and at least harvesting the lessons from those days can help you navigate future storms. Life will throw more at you. That's simply the way of things. The question is, are you more prepared this time? How would you carry yourself differently?

Spend some time thinking about this today, and jot down any notes or thoughts you come up with. It'll help adjust your perspective when it comes to future stressors and also help mend your relationship with time.

How?

Learning about our tendencies under duress gives us a chance to control the dial of our perception and avoid getting swept up in the white water of chaos. Even when things get crazy again, you can reach back to your experience of this event and draw wisdom from it. How shall you handle this one differently? Where do you refuse to go ever again? How can you maintain your calm and make better decisions this go-around?

These are things only you can answer. Those answers come from digging deep and learning lessons from your past.

DAY 86

time to read

Today we need to pull over and appreciate what reading can do for us. It creates *leverage*. Books take a person's life experience and distill it into salient lessons, stories, experiences, and anecdotes that can help us learn more about life. They take us into new corners of the world and give us information, insight, and knowledge.

Think about it. You are getting life experience in a digestible package. That means *real time spent* here on planet Earth by somebody who is now going to sum up, share, and package that experience for you.

It's like a compressed time packet that you get to glean wisdom from, with far less time invested. That's leverage.

All the most successful people I know are avid readers. They are committed to being lifelong learners and oftentimes have learned to speed-read to gain efficiency and maximize results. Does this sound crazy to you? Then know that most of these people also spend far more time chilling by the pool than your average person—and they're doing it while making themselves better.

Today grab a book you've been meaning to read and get in at least 30 pages. Relax into the process of learning from a book. It could be a novel, a historical tale, a self-help book, or whatever. Grab something that has been calling you, and make a point of fitting reading back into your life. Once you've made some space for books again, you'll begin to notice life's direction getting a bit more in focus. The more you read, the better off you are.

This is time well spent.

DAY 87

snack time

S nacks are great to keep our blood sugar stable. They help power our brains in between meals and give us the fuel we may need to stay aware and focused during our busy days. Today let's look at snacking and see if we can shift our perspective on it a bit.

It's easy to mindlessly power through a bag of whatever at our desk or in the car. Think about how often you blindly snack while doing something else. You may have been doing this for years; you may not even realize how much you're consuming, because it's become a reflex.

When we're unconscious of an activity, it draws us into a nebulous mental realm that's disconnected from the present moment. There's no connection between our eating and our hunger, and instead we end up falling into a reflexive habit of cramming all kinds of junk into our bodies without even realizing we're doing it.

Today we're breaking the habit of mindlessness during snack time. Whenever the moment comes that you're busting out the snack food—whether it's at the office, in a movie, or anywhere else—ask yourself what's in the food you're eating. It's easy to pay less attention to things we're shoveling in, but take a closer look. Is it clean? Is it natural? Is it good for you?

Next step: Are you appreciating it? We become unaware of the smell, texture, flavor, and temperature of a food as we engage in some other activity while eating. This is unconscious and certainly doesn't honor the life we're ingesting for our own gains. So take stock of the qualities so that you can be more aware when the pleasure starts to fade.

Now let's look at sheer volume. It's easy to go through a whole bag of chips or tub of ice cream while watching a show. It doesn't matter if they are pita chips or coconut ice cream with no sugar added. You're still dumping far too many calories into your system, and there's no amount of treadmill time today that can balance that load. How can you portion out the food that you're making available to yourself? Rather than bring out the whole bag, find a convenient single-serving container and put everything else away so that you don't even have the option of plowing through the whole amount.

After that, let's check in and see if you're chewing enough and slowing down to appreciate the food you're so lucky to have. Again, we go to some other place mentally while we scarf down a snack and hardly chew it enough to help our systems break it down. Chewing is an essential frontline step of digestion. You can use this snack time as a break, and you'll be surprised by how much you can learn about yourself when you're actually focusing on how eating makes you feel. You'll be so much more aware of when you're full or when the food becomes less enjoyable or even when your jaw starts to get sore from all of your chewing.

Today go through these motions every time you're getting a snack. Even if it's a handful of almonds you grabbed, slow down and take a minute to chew on them and savor them. This helps trigger satiety (so you'll snack less) and also helps you absorb and assimilate the food better. You can either take a conscious moment now on the front end or spend far more time breaking down the food or needing to work off the food later. What's it going to be?

DAY 88

time for your neighbors

When's the last time you hung out with your neighbors? Most of us quickly say hello and rush off to our crazy lives. A quick wave or smile and we're back in it.

Things didn't used to be this way. We knew the people around us and looked after them. They looked after our land, children, dogs, and mailboxes, and we returned the favor. We supported one another and acted like a community. Not today, not for many of us.

Make an effort today to simply connect with a neighbor. It may be hard, because they are also incredibly busy and are accustomed to jamming right by you, but *make the effort*. You don't need to stop someone's day for 20 minutes, but simply lean into the interaction for a moment. Put some intent and energy into it.

How? Let's start with eye contact and an enthusiastic hello. Ask how she is doing and tell her it is nice to see her. She may be in a rush, so don't make it weird. Just present yourself with some available energy and connect with her like a human would if she weren't in a panicked frenzy.

Maybe you suggest she comes over for some tea with her family later this week. Maybe you walk to the park together later, have a movie night, or go out for dinner—whatever's appropriate.

The point is to connect with the people around us and step out of the zombie-slave rushed mentality of our modern world. Stop time and do them the honor of acknowledging them. That may be all you get today, but it sets a precedent for future encounters. Chances are, with a gesture like this, they may come back with a much-needed smile later this month when you really need one.

We tend to ignore the people closest to us and take them for granted. Not today. Notice the people on your block and think about how you've engaged with them as a neighbor. Are you a good one, or are you too "doing that thing" by acting too busy for the people around you? It's okay: We've all fallen into the frenzy of modern times, but coming back is easy. It takes one person, namely YOU, to reach across the divide and bring both of you back to the present moment.

Don't know what to say? Simple. Acknowledge something in the natural environment that you're both standing in. Hey, those leaves look beautiful; amazing sunset; nice wind; check out those birds— whatever. Nature is *real,* and it is an anchor back into the present moment. It'll bring you both back to share an authentic moment and enjoy it. You can go back to your life from there, but this practice will build a good habit that can grow and flourish.

The goal is to stop time and simply enjoy a moment with a neighbor. You'll find yourself doing it more often, and someday you may even feel like you live in a solid neighborhood with lovely people all around you. These are good things. It is on us to make time for them.

DAY 89

utter relaxation

Have you ever experienced a state of utter relaxation? This means having no anxiety, trepidation, worries, concerns, or feelings of time compression. Some people have never felt safe enough to let go into this. It may be from early childhood events, having survived a war, or maybe living in a rough neighborhood. There are lots of reasons why we can't relax, and they are getting in the way of our greatness.

Letting go is an essential part of finding ourselves. We need to tap into our inner power, but there's something that gets in the way. It nags. It feels like a jittery state that can't quite unplug. You may feel it as muscle tension in your shoulders or jaw. Some feel it in the back of their neck. Many get tightness in the abdomen or chest.

Where do you feel it?

Have you ever stopped to confront this feeling? Have you ever paid close attention to it and honored it for what it is and why it is there? That's today's practice.

Let's turn our attention inward to the places in our body that are reluctant to let go. Lie down and take several breaths down to your lower abdomen. Breathe slowly down to that area and inflate it like a balloon. Work to relax your entire body from head to toe, and take a few minutes to settle in and feel nice and heavy.

Now let's scan your body for places of resistance. Instead of trying to "do something" to them, let's play a different game. When you encounter a tight area, breathe to it and then ask it why it can't relax. This may seem crazy, but you'll soon learn that ignoring your body is far less sane.

Ask your body why it is holding on to tension or resistance there.

Keep breathing to that area and see what comes up. Did a certain memory bubble up? Was there an injury that took place? Did you suddenly remember a childhood fear that's all too familiar?

Ask and be patient. It may be hard to put into words, but make sure you stay connected to your breathing and allow the feeling your body tries to convey to come up. Sense it and keep feeling it. It takes some time to get into a rhythm where we can trust the information coming back from our bodies as authentic and not mental chatter. Relax into this. Once there, simply *stay* with the feeling. Explore the spaciousness on the other side of resistance.

The challenge is one of polarity. We've moved *away* from the feelings of discomfort our whole lives. We've left these areas to gather energetic cobwebs and grow stale. Moving away from the discomfort has not served us. It is time to lean in.

Breathe to the area and relax deeply. Whatever feelings, emotions, or thoughts that come up are natural. They've been harbored in your tissue for years. Allow them to express and move through you. They needn't hide anymore. Let them go.

The more you accept, the more deeply you can relax into a perfectly still space. The more you can allow for this, the better you'll become at stopping time. Only by truly letting go can we tap into the eternal time that rejuvenates and restores us.

You can't drag the past much longer. Face it and accept it so you can release and let go.

DAY 90

turning the light of
awareness inward

A central tenet of my Taoist Alchemical system (theurbanmonk
.com/about/) is learning how to turn the light of awareness
around to observe the true self. This is the ultimate practice
in learning how to stop time. Your true self doesn't exist in time; your
true self sits on the perch of infinity and is in all places at all times.
This is the great secret of the mystics. Hearing it isn't enough, though.
So many people are infected by spiritual consumerism and go off
thinking, "Okay, okay, I've heard that. Give me something new."
That's the mark of the beast. Having a slight intellectual grasp of a
concept and thinking you've got it is a fatal spiritual flaw, one that's
infected the New Age movement and led to egotism and attitudes of
spiritual superiority.

The *experience* of this timelessness is the most transformative
moment of one's life. Getting there takes lots of practice, and most
New Age spiritual jargon is designed to sell you tricks that help cut
corners. There are no corners to cut. The whole thing is round.

Today let's take a dive inward. Find a quiet, dark place where you
can be uninterrupted for 15 to 20 minutes. Get comfortable, and sit
with your spine straight.

Start to breathe deeply down to your lower abdomen. Take a

couple of minutes and anchor the breath down low. This helps stabilize the mind and anchor it in our bioelectric field.

From here, focus our attention on the third eye. This is the space between your eyes at the front of your forehead. On the inhale, bring white light to the area, and on the exhale, have that white light shine outward in all directions. Take a few breaths doing this. Feel the pulse of the light in and out of the forehead.

On the next exhale, move a ball of light outward in front of your forehead about 6 inches. On the inhale, stabilize this ball and breathe more white light to it. On the next exhale, transfer your awareness from your forehead into the ball of light. On the next inhale, focus on turning your awareness back inward toward your forehead. Look back inside (from 6 inches in front of you).

Keep your awareness in the ball in front of you, and stay in this practice for a few minutes. Your awareness is resting in the ball of light looking back inward into your forehead. Hang here and try to stay with it. It is easy to get distracted—there's a lot of training that goes into holding this focus. Get a glimpse. Look inside with the light of your awareness and see what you *see*.

When you're ready to wrap up, on the next inhale, pull your awareness back into your forehead. Breathe white light back into it and have it expand in all directions on the exhale. Keep the focus inward and breathe to this energy center for a couple more minutes.

When you're ready to end the exercise, simply put your left palm on top of your forehead with your right palm over it and take a couple more solidifying breaths (palms facing in). Open your eyes and see how you feel.

DAY 91

stretching out trapped time

Today we unwind.

Life's compressive pressures end up registering in our bodies, and after a few decades, they seem to take up permanent residence. It may be in our neck, hips, lower back, or maybe those hamstrings that always seem to be tight.

Think of your body like a spring that is supposed to unload when released from pressure. Have you been loading it for so long that it seems stuck in a tight position? Do you walk around tense, ready to pop? It is common.

Maybe your head is now jutted forward because of stiff upper traps.

Maybe your pelvis is tilted from too much sitting.

Your knees may hurt from trying to run with a weak core.

There are lots of ways we compound physical trauma in our tissue, but how many ways do we release it?

The sad fact is that we seldom do. An occasional massage certainly helps, and when things have gone too far, we may be sent for some physical therapy. But by then, it's usually a pretty bad tendency, like a loaded coil about to discharge.

Developing a culture of stretching starts to take a bite out of this. Every minute spent stretching is like time travel. You get to go back to an incident, impact, stressor, or reaction you had in time and release it. The body will register stressors in our tissue, and we're living proof that these things don't release well on their own. We accumulate these little microtraumas until whole muscle chains develop new tendencies.

Just a few minutes of this daily routine will start to turn the tide. If you're really beat up, a massage, PT, acupuncture, or orthopedics may still be on the menu, but today we step in and take things into our own hands.

Time spent breathing into our body is a great investment. Stretching and opening up tight body parts releases trapped tension and trauma from a past time, which frees us from it in *current time*.

Think about it. That nagging stiff back may have started a few years ago or maybe crept up slowly, but whatever its origin, *it is here with you now and slowing down your present*. In fact, the loaded tissue is like energetic inertia that's keeping you from fully living and expressing movement in life today.

Stretching helps clear this anchor to the past. It releases the energy that's trapped in the tissue and helps us come to the present. It puts us in our bodies and helps us become more aware of our current state. Once we start to release certain muscle groups, we feel better but also become more aware of how we may have gotten there. We change our stride, fix our posture, swap our chair, or remember to stretch before running. It breeds awareness that helps prevent further (or future) compression.

Life's compressive forces keep us down. They keep us wound down and unable to fully express in the present moment. Releasing these energies frees us from yesterday's burdens and allows us to live freely in the present. I'd say that's time well spent.

Today start with stretching your hamstrings by folding forward and bending at the hips. Do this for a couple of minutes and then drop to one knee and lunge forward (one side at a time), stretching the front of your hips. Do this for 2 minutes on each side. From there, put one hand on a wall and open outward to stretch your chest. Do this for a minute and switch sides. Next, start to rotate your neck around in one direction and then the opposite. Slow down and ease through the parts that are stuck and crunchy.

Finally, feel for any other stuck parts of your body and stretch through them. You'll know where to go. In fact, your body can't wait to release and unwind. Spend some time and let it.

DAY 92

traumatic events

Have you ever noticed how particular traumatic events in your past carry a certain weight in your mental timeline? They imprint on our memory (and in the cells of our bodies) and hold an emotional charge that binds us to the event. If you imagine a timeline with a series of plus signs, a traumatic event is an imprint of a minus sign that then flips the plus signs from the time of the event forward.

Today when you experience an uncomfortable feeling that's associated with a harsh memory, close your eyes and trace back on the timeline to see what this looks like. Is there a flip in polarity from the time of the event that can be traced all the way back to the present moment? This is common.

Alfred Korzybski wrote of this in *Science and Sanity*. His groundbreaking work teaches us to go back to the original event and heal it there, where and when it happened. If you're worried about how you can access this, follow your emotions in. Go back to the memory and see what emotions it elicits. This may be uncomfortable, but stay with it. Breathe deeply and see where you feel the emotion in your body. Try to breathe to the area in your body where you feel the emotion. See where you are stuck.

Part of you has never left there or then. It keeps us bound to that energy and *that time* so we're never totally present in our lives. How can we be *here* if we're stuck *there*? How can we be in the *now* if we're partially parked in the *then*?

We can't. That's where a tremendous amount of our energy goes. That's where we leak today's energy into yesterday's drama.

Let's reclaim this. Spend some time reaching back in your memory, and search for places and times where you feel you got stuck. How can you heal the original event? Travel back in your mind's eye and put yourself back in that scenario. Watch it happen, but this time, *freeze the scene* and bathe it with love. Then *rewrite the scene* the way you would have liked for it to go. You can do this. Go back and forgive, heal, and create a new outcome at that moment, and then trace back from the traumatic event *toward the present moment* and clear any other energy that may be holding you back.

You may find that there are chains of events or incidents that carry the same flavor. These are often influenced by the distorted energy of the original event and also need to be healed. This takes a fair amount of practice but is extremely liberating. Once you get the hang of this, you'll find multiple places in your psyche where you've been stuck in a past time when some emotional trauma imprinted its energy on you.

This may seem like a lot of work, but the real work is carrying this burden around with you all day every day. Go back and clean up your timeline today. You'll feel a ton lighter.

DAY 93

you'll be pushing up flowers

Have you ever thought about what will happen to your body when you've passed? In the old days, there was a saying: "You'll be pushing up flowers." That's because people were buried in the ground, and everything except their bones would decompose and feed the life all around them. Today we use concrete around our caskets or incinerate our dead, but the principle remains the same.

When we're done, we're done. Our spirits return to the Eternal Flame, but our bodies become food for the life all around us. The earth eats us. Bacteria, *Protozoa,* nematodes, viruses, and many more organisms feast on the biomass that used to be us. Sound creepy? Sorry, that's reality.

So how do we interface with the reality of our mortality?

We stop and appreciate the time that we're given. The world could explode tomorrow. People get hit by buses. Death is always around the corner. So how are you living life?

Thinking about death shouldn't make you depressed. It should help build enthusiasm for the time you have here—to optimize it and savor every moment.

What does this have to do with flowers? A lot.

How pure was your body when it was laid to rest? Think ahead and see this one through. Was it filled with junk food, mercury, toxic makeup, and nasty chemicals? Is that what you'd like to feed the pretty flowers that flourish off of your body? I'm not sure they'd flourish.

Before we went crazy with our "innovations" in chemistry, most of what we ate, produced, and put on our skin was natural. That meant there wasn't a toxic impact on us and the planet. Today things are different. Would you be proud of the organic fuel you put back into the earth, or are you glowing in the dark?

Now is the time to think about this and make a change. You can cleanse your liver, detox heavy metals out of your brain and bones, purge chemicals out of your diet and household items, and, frankly, come clean in a few months. What would a pure version of you look and feel like? What impact would that have on the planet and generations to come? If those flowers over your grave were edible, would you want your great-grandchildren eating them?

You're not here for just you. You are part of a vast ecosystem, and your time is borrowed. Today think about your footprint on Earth and how you could clean it up. The chemicals stop being made if nobody buys them. What can you do right now to positively impact your legacy on the planet?

What would the flowers look like in the ecosystem of your life? How clean is the wake behind you?

Today make the changes upstream. Clean up what goes in your body and on your skin. This is a revolutionary act that will transform the planet.

DAY 94

time lost

Although there's no use crying over spilled milk, there certainly is an opportunity to reflect and see how you could have avoided that incident for the future. That's the deal with lost time. You are not getting it back, but there's a lesson packed in there that can be quite educational.

We lose time every day. Whether it is in leaving the house 10 minutes late and hitting the worst of the traffic or blanking and missing our exit, there are plenty of hours that we bemoan losing to the road.

What about time looking for something? You can spend cumulative hours looking for things that have gone missing in your house. The time is gone, and if the item doesn't turn up, it leaves an open loop in your mind and elevates your stress.

Let's look at where you've been losing time lately. Look back at the past month or so of your life and think about lost time. What happened in these incidents? Were you careless or unfocused about what you wanted to get done and when? Did you have bad boundaries? How committed were you to accomplishing the task? Did you end up in a social situation that dragged on? Run through all the examples of lost time that come up and list them for a few minutes. Reach back and pull out the instances when you can recall being particularly frustrated about having to wait around. How much time do you think you've lost to the items that you listed?

Once you have the list, let's now look at ways you could have avoided this situation. Were you careless with boundaries? Did you forget your other commitments? Was there some socially awkward reason why you didn't speak up or simply leave?

There are numerous reasons we get stuck and lose valuable time in things that don't deserve it. Today's task is to pick one chronic source of time loss in your life and make a plan to thwart it. Look into where you could reabsorb some of that lost time *in the future* by understanding your tendencies and learning where you need to get tighter on controls. This doesn't mean being a jerk if you have a slow-moving person in your life who tends to hold you up. It means planning ahead to figure out what you can do to change the situation for the better and also how you can alter your planning to accommodate inevitable forces that always slow you down.

Look at where you've lost time lately and learn your lessons. That time is lost, but next go-round, have the clarity not to make the same mistake again.

DAY 95

creative time

Have you ever noticed how you can't force creative time? One must often wait until the muse is upon you, but what if you need to draw on your creativity today? How can you go there if you technically can't force it? Let's practice.

Creativity comes when our heart center and our third eye are open. These energy centers tend to shut down when stress is getting the best of us. Sadly, that's far too often for most people. It leads to a sour mood and grants less access to the creative juices that come from a more relaxed state of being.

Another issue comes from trying to be creative instead of slipping into a state of receptivity. You can't "do" creativity, but you can allow for it. The challenge here is to avoid the mindset that says, "Okay, now let's get creative." That doesn't work. Relax into your primordial state and *allow* for it. This may not happen abruptly. You're now trying to access a different quality of time that has its own rules. Enter respectfully.

Here's today's practice.

Take deep breaths down to your lower dantian (3 inches below your navel in the center of your body). Relax and settle in for 2 to 3 minutes, letting your breathing slow down. Observe the breath as it passes through the center of your body, gently inflating and deflating your lower abdomen.

From here, move your focus to your heart. Feel it warm up and glow with each inhale, and then allow that warmth to spread through your entire body with each exhale. Do this for several minutes. Put a smile on your face and keep your eyes closed. Take slow, deep, meaningful breaths and allow your breath to soften your chest cavity.

Now try to maintain this type of breathing while opening your eyes and taking a walk. Stay in this mindset and enjoy the world around you. Keep that smile on your face and keep circulating warmth throughout your body. That's it. Don't try to pivot and extract data immediately. Ease into this space and get comfortable there. If something genius comes up, go ahead and write it down or take a voice note in your phone.

The key is to not get right back into your head. This type of breathing helps engage the right hemisphere of your brain, which allows for creativity. Don't let your logical mind slam back in and crowd it out. Creativity *emerges* from this space. You need to get comfortable here and allow the creative juices to spring up naturally. The rational mind creates a container that can be helpful, but it often gets in our way. We may have imposed rules, bumpers, and regulations that keep us confined in our thinking and out of our creative mind. Drop into your heart and access that energy. Let it blossom like a flower, and give it space. Creativity will soon follow.

Over time, you'll have more access to this space, and if you remain respectful of its different quality of time, you can reap tremendous benefits from it in your life.

DAY 96

time with the stars

Our ancestors grew up looking at the stars nightly, oftentimes for hours. When is the last time you gazed up at the night sky? Better yet, when's the last time you slept under the stars? It has become quite uncommon for city dwellers to even see them, let alone slow down to enjoy them.

Our ancestors created amazing stories around the constellations, and they used them for practical purposes. From navigation to the shift in seasons, there's a critical matrix of data up there that helped us plant harvests, sail boats, and establish religious ceremonies. It was always a big deal, but now the stars are in Hollywood and we watch them on TV. This is tragic.

Tonight get outside and spend some time looking up. If you live in a bright city, consider driving to a vantage point where you can at least see more than at home.

Plan on spending at least 30 minutes doing this. Take warm clothes if you live in a cold climate.

Sit down or lie flat on your back, soften your gaze, and look up at the stars all around you. You could try to identify the things you know and recognize up there or simply enjoy the speckled view. Breathe deeply down to your lower abdomen and connect your breathing with what you're seeing. Sync up with the sky.

Your gong tonight is to identify three constellations in the sky. There are plenty of apps that can help you do this. I like Starwalk, as it's tied to GPS and will help you track the stars in real time in the night sky. Once you've identified them, read up on them. See what the ancients said about your three new friends. Learn the names of the stars within them if you'd like.

Here's the crazy part: Almost everything you're seeing up there is not in the present. You are looking into the *past*. It takes the light from many of those stars millions of years to get to the earth, and what you're seeing is light from ancient days. Humans have been around for a few thousand years by contrast. You personally? Maybe a few decades. The known universe is billions of years old. Think about that for a minute. Gaze up into the black night sky and think about where you are sitting right now in the vast expanse of space and time. It is so big that it's hard to grasp, but it is there. Actually, if you're fortunate enough to see a clear night sky, it is *everywhere*.

We're surrounded by the enormity of the entire universe, and the light waves that are bathing you right now are coming from ancient times. You are effectively looking into space and *through time*. How much does what your coworker said today weigh up against your view right now? How significant is your life? What can you do in the next couple decades to leave your mark here on this planet before being absorbed back into the vast expanse of this eternal canvas above you? We all come from the explosion of these stars above you, and one day, probably in a long time, our atoms will be floating back out there.

Take a moment and weigh your daily problems against the scale of what's above you, and recalibrate a bit. The universe is big, and time is so vast we can hardly grasp it. Does it not make sense to take a few minutes to enjoy life a bit more today?

DAY 97

eye contact and face time

In the old days, when we engaged in a conversation, we experienced a lot of eye contact. There's a tremendous amount of nonverbal communication that happens in any human encounter, and eye contact is a big part of that. The eyes are considered the window to the soul, and we can tell a lot about a person—how she's feeling, how trustworthy she is, and much more—when we look into her eyes.

In the modern world, much of this is lost, as people are scattered. More of our conversations take place through a keyboard than in person. Even when we're in the same room as our companion, our eyes are constantly scanning from side to side as we're overwhelmed by electronics and digital screens. It leads to choppy conversations, superficial relationships, and lonely people.

We've evolved over tens of thousands of years to connect with people with genuine face time. Now that's an app. While helpful, nothing truly replaces close human contact and eye-to-eye engagement. Just because the world has gotten ludicrous, it doesn't mean we have to be. Bringing back our humanity doesn't take much. We need to slow down and connect with others. We need to touch another human soul by reaching across the room and *seeing* them truly with our eyes. Look deep inside and discover the people around you. There's a lot more to them than what they say and how they act. Their true self is right there.

Today make a point of connecting with everyone you see by using strong eye contact. This doesn't mean flashing them with your high beams and weirding them out. It means holding soft yet sincere eye contact that's backed by a warm smile; a friendly remark might also feel natural. You'll notice a number of things throughout the day as you do this.

Some people get downright uncomfortable with it. Take a note of this, and don't let it dissuade you. Some people will be touched, and it will immediately slow them down and remind them of what's real. A few may be taken aback and get teary-eyed. That's how long it's been since they've had real human contact.

You may also find that some people in your life are totally normal and amazed that you've shown up. Don't be shocked if you find that you're the disconnected one in the room who's now coming to life.

This exercise brings you into the present and connects you with people on an emotional level. This is a powerful space outside the onslaught of the day's stressors. It's a reprieve from the hectic parade you're on, an authentic moment you share with another human being. Take the time to do this throughout the day today and log some mental notes of what you notice.

Look inside them and you'll find something you weren't expecting: *yourself.* To truly love and acknowledge others is a pure path to finding oneself. Take the time today and connect. This magically stops time and brings us into a sacred space. Savor it.

DAY 98

boredom

When's the last time you were bored? For some, boredom is never an issue: They hardly have time to get to their myriad interests. That may not be you, though. There are millions of people who are bored out of their minds every day. Is that possibly you?

Let's dive into boredom today, because it's an interesting stance, kind of like a place where your interface with time has gone awry. Most people who are bored have suppressed their desires for so long that they feel trapped in a life that lacks any enthusiasm. Maybe during childhood, you wanted to go out and play but were forced to sit and practice piano. Now you resent it. Perhaps you love the outdoors but had to take a "job job" to pay the bills and got lulled into a dreary sleep. Maybe you're depressed and feel no spark for anything. That's also common.

Regardless of where you stand with boredom, today's exercise is to get realigned with what you want to be doing with your life and find a way to integrate it into the life that you have no matter what. What did you enjoy doing as a young child? Where did you like to go and why? What used to impress or intrigue you and make you smile? Chances are you'll still enjoy such things.

Spend some time thinking about what truly brings you joy and then think about the last time you did it. Is it art? Sports? Cooking? For some it may be decades since they've last tried it. That's what life does to us sometimes. We get carried away on the ship we're on and years later find ourselves in a far-off land with strangers whom we can't relate to. We're tired and lonely and call that feeling bored. It's much worse than that. It is a fundamental misalignment of your soul with the time that you were given. Nothing is a bigger slap in the face of God than a human wasting their life away somewhere without passion.

You need a spark. Where did it used to come from? How can you find something that brings joy back to you and make time in your life for it again? It is your time. Sure, you may work for someone during the day, but you have plenty of you time that can be directed toward something you're passionate about.

What is it?

Keep digging and asking. Try new things and test your assumptions. Look at life through the eyes of a Martian and take all of your current circumstances off the table. If you could do anything you wanted in the world, what would it be? Great. Now start rowing in that direction.

Today's practice is to simply spend some time thinking about this and writing down places where you left your joy and forgot to have fun. Boredom is a symptom of our misalignment. Connect your heart back with what used to make you passionate, and bring back the joy. Dig!

DAY 99

waiting

Today we're going to gain a lot of ground. Our lesson is a simple hack that'll radically transform your attitude toward time. It has to do with the idea that you will learn to *never wait again*.

What does this mean?

For starters, it does NOT mean to fill every down moment by staring at your mobile device. Shit happens. People are late. Traffic is everywhere, and things are not perfect. That's the world we live in. Things don't always go our way.

And what do we do in these circumstances? We fester, we swear, we get antsy, and we fume.

How helpful is that?

Today's plan is to catch yourself every time you're presented with an *opportunity* to wait and redirect the energy to something positive. If you're at a restaurant and they say the food is 5 minutes late, your attitude should be "Great! The universe just *gifted me* 5 minutes!" This may mean a few things:

- More quality time with the person you're sitting with
- A few minutes to breathe deeply down to your lower abdomen and relax your system
- Time to journal and jot down some thoughts
- Time to read or listen to an audiobook or podcast
- Time to think

The moral of the story is to *take ownership of your time*. Never let anyone or any circumstance waste your time again. You don't need to fill every moment of your waking life with productivity and distraction. You don't need anything at all when you learn to meditate. Even in a public place, you can do some deep breathing to your lower abdomen and nourish your spirit while sitting there. This way there's no angst over waiting time: It becomes "found time" to catch your breath and dive deeply into a relaxed state.

Not feeling like you need to chill out? Fine. Stretch. Do some pushups, call Mom, or whatever.

It is your time. Take ownership of it today and then make this exercise a lifelong habit.

DAY 100

time ROI

In business there's a concept called return on investment, or ROI, for short. The principle is simple: There should be a reward for resources invested in a given venture. Today let's think about this in the context of time. Where is your time being invested, and are you happy with the returns?

What are the current results you are having in life? Think about this in relation to your desires, goals, and aspirations. How do you spend the majority of your time, and how closely does that align with the value of those activities? Are you feeling closer or more distant from the things or experiences you long for? If your time spent isn't resulting in the life you want, then we have a lot to work with. Today let's do an assessment of where your time is going and whether you think there may be better ways to spend it.

Look through your calendar and make note of the things you do that don't result in an outcome you care about. If you're doing something unhealthy such as smoking or eating junk food, well, that's an obvious place to start. After that, start to look at the things you don't enjoy doing. Those are the ones that drag down your quality of life. Are these items absolutely necessary? Many may be for now, but how can you shift your life so that you can better enjoy your time? I'm not talking about quitting a job that you need or not attending events that are incredibly important to your loved ones, but is there a way to shift the energy that you're dedicating to tasks you don't love so you have more bandwidth left for the things you do?

Can you reabsorb some time that's being wasted on activities you don't enjoy? How about time on the road? Maybe a carpool or public transit can free up some time. Perhaps you can ride your bike to work and check off the exercise tab while you're at it.

Today, look at the amount of fulfillment, joy, fitness, money, or whatever other measurement that makes sense to get out of your actions. We work for money. How can you maximize time in for money out? Exercise is great. Can you get more gains for the same amount of time in? For example, if you're used to spending half an hour on the treadmill watching a show, can you do some high-intensity work for that half hour and reap better rewards? Leave no stone unturned today. Look at everything.

You want to make the most of the time you spend on this planet, and we all live on *borrowed time*. If you're investing what you have in a given activity, imagine looking back a few years from now. Would you think this was time well spent? If not, then stop wasting your life force on it now. It's that simple. Fast forward a few years and look back. Would you be happy with where you spent today's time? What long-term return do you see it providing you?

The challenge with time poverty is our own belief systems. What is running through your mind that creates scarcity and inefficiency in your life? Challenge those beliefs, and take ownership of how you spend your time. The results will be magnificent.

CONCLUSION

STEPPING INTO TIME PROSPERITY

Time is a majestic and powerful force that is the currency of life. We can either be slaves to its relentless march, or we can step in and master it. The art of stopping time and cultivating time prosperity gives us *agency* in our lives. We stop feeling out of control, and we clean up the mess that drives our anxiety and insomnia. We find time prosperity by trimming the waste and savoring the moments we have to catch our breath. We let go of where we're frivolous, and we lean into the things that are life-enhancing and enriching.

Now that you've completed the 100-Day Gong, you will feel harmony with the time in which you live. You've been given lots of things to think about and numerous practices to help you master time each day. There's plenty of work left to do, and you'll need to be meticulous about minding your time. Sometimes things will be fast and you will need to ride with them. At other times, you will need to power down and slow down. But regardless, being in sync with the rhythms of nature will help you find harmony. Let's align with this powerful wave and learn to surf with it.

Take your notes from the past 100 days and review them now. Where have you been, and how far have you come? What did you realize that you've since forgotten, and how can you get back on track?

Moving forward, apply these filters to your time each day. Look at where you can pull the nectar out of life and use time as your greatest ally. We don't know how much of it we have, but we can choose to make the most of what we've been given. Invest your time in your legacy, your family, and an enriching experience here on planet Earth. Learn to look through the lens of this book and pull maximum life value from your time.

Live a life of time prosperity that is enriching, supportive, and regenerative.

Are you ready for more?

I invite you to now reread this book out of order. Basically, pick it up and open to a different chapter daily. I call it Gong Roulette. Each lesson will bring more clarity and value to you. Keep working toward time prosperity and you'll find more energy, clarity, and happiness along the way.

Enjoy,
Pedram Shojai

ACKNOWLEDGMENTS

I'm eternally grateful to my lineage for the wisdom that's been passed on through me. Dr. Carl Totton has been a friend, teacher, mentor, and advocate since I stumbled into his Kung Fu studio as a young man. Dr. Thomas McCombs has been an amazing uncle and teacher along the way. The passing of GM Share Lew has fortunately left some excellent torch bearers for the world. I'm honored to be in such esteemed company.

My wife has been my partner and ally along the way. She's been a wonderful mother and partner and has allowed me the time and space to take on big projects like this. Sol and Sophia have been my inspiration; Buster and Sunshine, my furry companions and best friends.

A special thanks goes out to Nick Polizzi, Kevin Gianni, Leanne Ely, Jeff Hays, Michael Lovitch, Hollis Carter, JJ Virgin, Dave Asprey, Michael and Izabella Wentz, and a whole host of wonderful friends "in the business" who've been lovely and supportive along the way. We are stronger together, and I'm honored that you've always had my back.

I'm also doubly grateful to Mark van Wijk and Carl Lindahl who've helped blaze trails on the film side with me. What an adventure it has been, and you guys are amazing humans. Lorenzo Phan and Sean Rivas have provided priceless support and good vibes along the way. Bill Dodge has kept me sane and made things work. I'm very grateful to you all.

Last but certainly not least, I'm saving the biggest thanks for the family who made this all possible. Farhad and Sonbol Shojai, Homa Hamidi, Shery, Ali, Armin, Sharareh, and all the cousins. What's life without family? Growing up in our "small village" has given us the love, support, and sanity to be able to go out and do what we do. I love you all.

ABOUT THE AUTHOR

Pedram Shojai, OMD, is the *New York Times* bestselling author of *The Urban Monk,* the founder of Well.org, producer of the movies *Vitality, Origins,* and *Prosperity,* and the host of *The Urban Monk* podcast. An ordained priest of the Yellow Dragon Monastery in China, he is an acclaimed Qigong master, master herbalist, and Doctor of Oriental Medicine.